MW01533226

GOOD NEWS STUDIES

Consulting Editor: Robert J. Karris, O.F.M.

Other Titles in Preparation

Reckoning with Romans

A Contemporary Reading
of
Paul's Gospel

by

Brendan Byrne, S.J.

Michael Glazier
Wilmington, Delaware

About The Author

Brendan Byrne, S.J., is Professor of New Testament at Jesuit Theological College, within the United Faculty of Theology, Parkville, Melbourne, Australia. After early studies in Australia he pursued doctoral research at Oxford University. His dissertation, *'Sons of God' – 'Seed of Abraham'*, a study of Paul's description of Christians in terms of 'sons/children of God' against the Jewish background, was published in the series *Analecta Biblica* of the Pontifical Institute, Rome (No. 83; 1979). He contributes articles in the Pauline and Johannine area to journals in the United States, Britain and Australia. From 1978–1984 he was rector of the Jesuit house of studies, Campion College, Kew, Melbourne.

First published in 1986 by Michael Glazier, Inc. 1935 West Fourth Street, Wilmington, Delaware, 19805.©1986 by Michael Glazier, Inc.

Library of Congress Catalog Card Number: 86-45318
International Standard Book Numbers:
  Good News Studies: 0-89453-290-1
  Reckoning with Romans: 0-89453-585-4

Typography by Connie Runkel. Printed in the United States of America.

Table of Contents

Foreword

The late Bishop John Robinson made a perceptive comment concerning commentaries on biblical books. "I have vowed," he wrote, "never to write a biblical commentary. For in a commentary you have to say something on everything, whether you have anything to say or not." By that criterion this book is not a commentary. I do intend to work through the text of Romans, omitting only some material in the final chapters. But I shall certainly not have something to say on everything and will pass over many details which a commentator could not afford to ignore. What is offered here might best be described as a close reading of the text from a particular point of view.

That particular point of view arises out of what I believe to be Paul's central preoccupation in Romans: his proclamation of the gospel as the revelation of the righteousness or saving justice of God. Each document of the New Testament preserves an early Christian reflection upon the meaning of God's act in Jesus Christ. And each one casts that reflection in its own distinctive mould. To have discerned and articulated the contribution of each biblical author has been one of the chief tasks and achievements of New Testament scholarship in recent years. Paul's distinctive contribution, at least in Romans, is to present Jesus in terms of the "righteousness of God." For him Christ is the embodiment of God's saving fidelity to the world.

Such a presentation of Jesus may sound rather abstract compared to the more concrete portraits found in the Gospels and other New Testament writings. But in casting his gospel in these terms Paul applied to Jesus one of the richest concepts of the biblical tradition, one so central that in a sense it brings in its train the entire Old Testament revelation of God. The concept of "righteousness" carries with it a whole pattern of association concerned with the enhancement and preservation of the social order in the context of human relationship with God. It holds together within one framework the "justice" or "righteousness" of God and the "justice" or right order of the world.

Such a perspective lends a particular relevance to Romans at the present time. The letter to Rome has always been a document of central importance in the Christian tradition. But one legacy of the Reformation controversy was an interpretation of "justification" as primarily concerned with God's designs upon the individual. The rediscovery of the rich Old Testament background to Paul's thought and in particular an awareness of his distinctive view of the "righteousness of God" has enabled us to grasp the wide social implications of his gospel. While Romans analyzes the individual human predicament with remarkable subtlety and penetration, it also presents a vision of human dignity and destiny in the wider context of God's future for the world. In view of this the letter gains fresh interest at a time when Christian communities are recognizing an intrinsic link between the promotion of justice and the preaching of the gospel.[1]

My aim in this book is to help the reader distil this vision from the text of Romans. While recognizing that there may be alternative and perhaps quite contrary interpretations, it is not my intention to argue every inch of the way, to contest every step of ground. I believe the interpretation to be exegetically sound in both detail and overall pattern. But I shall present it in positive fashion, allowing it to commend or not commend itself on its own merits. The goal is not to impose an understanding upon the reader, but rather to render a

---

[1]Cf. *Justice in the World,* Statement of Second Synod of Bishops, Rome, November 1971: "Action on behalf of justice and participation in the transformation of the world fully appear to us as a constitutive dimension of the preaching of the Gospel" (#6) (Text in J. Gremillion [ed.], *The Gospel of Peace and Justice* [New York: Orbis, 1976] 513-29); *Breaking Barriers: Official Report of the Fifth Assembly of the World Council of Churches: Nairobi 1975* (Ed. D. Paton, London/Grand Rapids: SPCK/Eerdmans, 1976) pp. 52-55, 231-36.

difficult text more accessible for personal appropriation.

Let us admit from the start: a "close reading" of the text will make demands upon the reader. Romans does not yield its riches without some pain and toil. Several years of teaching Paul to a wide variety of people in an ecumenical setting have convinced me, however, that for those who are prepared to make the effort the outcome is immensely rewarding. Not only do they obtain a grasp of Paul's greatest work. As the mature presentation of Paul's gospel, Romans opens the way to a rich understanding of his remaining letters, which shine the light of that gospel upon the more concrete situations of Christian life.

No small measure of the labor involved in studying Paul consists in the attempt to grasp his message "from the inside," to have a feel for the issues of Romans from within his own religious framework. This will involve extensive, but not, I trust, unattractive, forays into the *Old Testament background.* No less important is a solid consideration of the *apocalyptic world-view* of later Judaism; since this apocalyptic background is so central to the language and thought of Romans, I give an outline of it at some length in the Introduction. Within this overall perspective we shall attend carefully to Paul's distinctive *"language,"* that is, to the ways he uses terms such as "gospel," "salvation," "glory" and so forth. Such terms make up the familiar currency of religious discourse, well-worn and blunted by centuries of use. Appreciation of Romans is greatly enhanced when Paul's language is read in its original precision and sharpness.

Finally, I shall pay close attention to *structure* — the structure of the letter as a whole and that of the individual elements. Nothing makes a text yield its meaning so readily as a careful examination of its structure. To facilitate such analysis I have set out the relevant text in translation according to its structure at the head of each section. The translation is my own and, for the purpose of more accurate study, remains fairly literal.

In offering this interpretation of Romans I am naturally indebted to the work of many Pauline scholars in recent years. In particular I should like to single out the work of

Ernst Käsemann, whose understanding of the "righteousness of God" has dominated recent Pauline scholarship in such a rewarding and provocative way. Käsemann's writings, including his monumental *Commentary on Romans*,[2] are now for the most part available in English. Unfortunately, Ulrich Wilckens' three-volume commentary,[3] a landmark of ecumenical Pauline scholarship, remains untranslated. To the work of these two scholars I am indebted on almost every page. I should also like to acknowledge and recommend J.C. Beker's *Paul the Apostle*,[4] which has so notably drawn attention to the centrality of apocalyptic in Paul's language and thought.

At the close of each chapter, I give some indication of further reading which the reader might profitably pursue. Asterisks before items in these lists denote works of more immediate relevance and accessibility to the general reader. I have also included a small proportion of studies in languages other than English where such studies have notably contributed to the approach taken in this work. Reference to commentaries, however, has been omitted since their relevance at each particular stage is presupposed. An annotated list of commentaries immediately follows this Foreword, along with a selection of useful works in English on Paul.

In conclusion I must acknowledge my indebtedness to the Jesuit community of St. Aloysius' College, Sydney, who in the midst of their own heavy labors gave hospitality, companionship and leisure to one engaged in the far more sedentary pursuit of writing. Most of all perhaps I am indebted to several generations of students at the United Faculty of Theology, Parkville, Melbourne. Anything of value in what follows is due in great measure to the stimulus and questioning their interaction with Paul has provided.

Brendan Byrne, S.J.
Jesuit Theological College
United Faculty of Theology
Parkville, Melbourne

[2]Grand Rapids: Eerdmans, 1980.

[3]*Der Brief an die Römer,* EKK VI/1-3, Neukirchen/ Vluyn: Neukirchener Verlag, 1978-82.

[4]Philadelphia: Fortress, 1980.

Commentaries and Other Recommended Literature

RECOMMENDED COMMENTARIES

C.K. Barrett, *A Commentary on the Epistle to the Romans,* London: Black, 1957, reprinted 1972; San Francisco: Harper & Row, 1958.

[Most valuable. Discusses all issues with great clarity and conciseness. Becoming somewhat dated.]

M. Black, *Romans,* London: Oliphants, 1973; revised ed. Grand Rapids: Eerdmans, 1981.

[Presents essential information for the general reader; one misses a more ample discussion in several areas]

C.E.B. Cranfield, *The Epistle to the Romans* (ICC), 2 Vols., Edinburgh: Clark, 1975, 1979.

[Provides fair and exhaustive discussion of all details. Difficult to use without some knowledge of Greek.]

_____, *Romans: A Shorter Commentary,* Edinburgh: Clark, 1985; Grand Rapids: Eerdmans.

[A concise version of the two-volume commentary with much technical detail, including the Greek, omitted.]

C.H. Dodd, *The Epistle of Paul to the Romans,* London: Hodder & Stoughton, 1932, reprinted Collins, Fontana, 1959.

[Most readable introduction to Romans. Has rendered Paul intelligible to countless modern readers. Rather dated now.]

E. Käsemann, *Commentary on Romans,* Grand Rapids: Eerdmans, 1980.

[The layout and constant engagement with controversy do not make for easy reading; but immensely stimulating and provocative.]

O. Kuss, *Der Römerbrief. Übersetzt und erklärt,* 3 Vols., Regensburg: Pustet, 1957, 1959, 1978.

[Outstanding commentary from a great Pauline scholar of the Catholic tradition. Very valuable excursuses on questions of key theological interest.]

U. Wilckens, *Der Brief an die Römer,* 3 Vols., Cologne/ Neukirchen-Vluyn: Benziger/Neukirchener, 1978, 1980, 1982.

[Comprehensive commentary, with rich theological reflection from an ecumenical standpoint. Contains full bibliography and many valuable excursuses.]

OTHER HELPFUL LITERATURE

On Romans:

P.J. Achtemeier, *Romans,* Interpretation, Atlanta: John Knox, 1985.

C.K. Barrett, *Reading Through Romans,* London: Epworth, 1963.

*K.P. Donfried (ed.), *The Romans Debate,* Minneapolis: Augsburg, 1977.

A. Feuillet, "Romains (Épître aux)," *Supplement au Dictionnaire de la Bible* (Paris: Letouzey et Ané, 1928-) Fasc. 56-57 (1982-83) Cols. 739-863.

*J.A.T. Robinson, *Wrestling with Romans,* London: SCM, 1979; Philadelphia: Fortress.

Survey Articles: W.S. Campbell, "The Romans Debate," *Journal for the Study of the New Testament* 10 (1981) 19-28; idem, "Revisiting Romans," *Scripture Bulletin,* 12 (1981) 2-10.

Interpretation 34/1 (January 1980) [Entire issue devoted to Romans.]

On Paul more generally:

C.K. Barrett, *Essays on Paul,* London: SPCK, 1982; Philadelphia: Westminster.

*_____, *From First Adam to Last: A Study in Pauline Theology,* London: Black, 1962; New York: Scribners.

*J.C. Beker, *Paul the Apostle: The Triumph of God in Life and Thought,* Philadelphia: Fortress, 1980; London: SCM.

*G. Bornkamm, *Paul,* New York: Harper & Row, 1971; London: Hodder & Stoughton.

*R. Bultmann, *Theology of the New Testament* (2 vols.; London: SCM, 1952, 1955; New York: Scribners, 1955) Volume 1.

*B.J. Byrne, *'Sons of God' — 'Seed of Abraham': A Study of the Idea of the Sonship of God of all Christians in Paul against the Jewish Background,* Rome: Biblical Institute, 1979.

N.A. Dahl, *Studies in Paul: Theology for the Early Christian Mission,* Minneapolis: Augsburg, 1977.

*W.D. Davies, *Paul and Rabbinic Judaism,* 4th ed., Philadelphia: Fortress, 1980; London: SPCK.

W.G. Doty, *Letters in Primitive Christianity,* Philadelphia: Fortress, 1973.

*J.A. Fitzmyer, *Pauline Theology: A Brief Sketch,* Englewood Cliffs, NJ: Prentice-Hall, 1967.

*M.D. Hooker, *Pauline Pieces,* London: Epworth, 1979. Published in the USA as *A Preface to Paul,* New York: Oxford University, 1980.

*E. Käsemann, *Perspectives on Paul,* Philadelphia:Fortress, 1971; London: SCM [A collection of articles, mainly on Romans.]

L. Keck, *Paul and his Letters,* Philadelphia: Fortress, 1980.

*W.A. Meeks, *The First Urban Christians. The Social World of the Apostle Paul,* New Haven-London: Yale University, 1983.

J. Murphy-O'Connor, *Becoming Human Together: The Pastoral Anthropology of St. Paul,* 2nd ed., Wilmington: Glazier, 1982.

E.P. Sanders, *Paul and Palestinian Judaism,* Philadelphia: Fortress, 1977; London: SCM.

A. Schweitzer, *The Mysticism of Paul the Apostle,* New York: Holt, 1931; London: Black.

R. Scroggs, *Paul for a New Day,* Philadelphia: Fortress, 1977.

*W.D. Stacey, *The Pauline View of Man,* London: Macmillan, 1956.

*K. Stendahl, *Paul among Jews and Gentiles and Other Essays,* Philadelphia: Fortress, 1977; London: SCM.

*M.J. Taylor (ed.), *A Companion to Paul: Readings in Pauline Theology,* New York: Alba House, 1975 [A collection of key articles on Paul in abridged and simplified form.]

Introduction

Before entering upon study of the text of Romans, I propose to discuss three topics which the overall interpretation will presuppose: 1. The Occasion and Purpose of the Letter; 2. The Apocalyptic Background to Paul's Thought; 3. The Structure of the Letter as a whole.

The Occasion and Purpose of Romans

It is generally agreed that Paul wrote Romans during an extended stay in Corinth just prior to setting out for Jerusalem with the collection for the "saints" gathered from the Gentile churches (cf. Acts 20:1-4,16; 2 Corinthians 8-9; Rom 15:25). His task in Jerusalem achieved, Paul hoped to carry on his preaching in the West, specifically in Spain, passing through Rome on the way (Rom 15:28-29). In terms of absolute chronology the stay in Corinth fell somewhere between the years 53-57 C.E. A good case can be made out for the early months of 57 C.E.

But why precisely did Paul write to the Christian community at Rome, a community which he himself had not founded? And why did he write a letter containing a long and systematic exposition of the gospel to an extent quite unprecedented in his earlier writings? These questions have been the subject of much discussion in recent years. Since the issue does have some bearing upon the interpretation at various points, I give some outline of it here.

The fact that systematic exposition of the gospel makes up so large a part of Romans has given rise to the long-standing view that, in contrast to the remaining letters, it is not addressed to a particular situation in the recipient community. On the contrary, Romans is more in the nature of a theological treatise, a kind of encyclical letter, meant to be read in several Pauline churches (the copy preserved being the one intended for Ephesus). For some scholars Romans represents Paul's "last will and testament." Or else it has been composed with the forthcoming visit to Jerusalem very much in mind and represents the defense or "apology" of his gospel which he knows he will be there called upon to give. This explains why it takes so much the form of a "dialogue with Jews."

In recent years, however, there has been renewed insistence that due weight be given to the particular situation of the Christian community in Rome when assessing the purpose and occasion of Romans. Scholars who make this point draw attention, in the first place, to the extended treatment of tolerance in the matter of food laws (14:1 - 15:13). The Christian community in Rome was a mixed one, made up of converts from both Jewish and Gentile backgrounds. That disputes should have broken out between those adhering to the strict Jewish practice and those (Gentiles and less rigorous Jews) favoring a more liberal approach would be quite likely. Trouble of this kind, reported to Paul, may well have occasioned the admonition given in these chapters.

But the passages which shed most light on the question are the introductory and concluding sections, 1:8-15 and 15:14-33 respectively. It is in these outer "frames," as it were, of the letter that Paul gives some account of his intentions, both in writing and in planning to visit. In the earlier passage he attests his long-cherished desire to visit the community and states his aim "to impart some spiritual gift for your strengthening" and "that we may be mutually encouraged by our common faith, yours and mine" (vv. 11-12). This tactful and rather modest statement is repeated in the following verses (vv. 13-15) in tones of far greater authority. Now, as apostle of the Gentiles, Paul wants to "reap some harvest" among the Romans in virtue of his "obligation" to Gentiles of all races. Finally, (v. 15) he states quite boldly his eagerness "to preach the gospel to you also who are in Rome." That is, Paul seems to understand the letter as amounting to a preaching of the gospel to the Romans, in virtue of his solemn responsibility as "apostle to the Gentiles."

In the concluding section (15:14-33) the statement of intent takes a somewhat different tack. Paul first of all concedes that he has written "rather boldly" (v. 15) to the Romans in virtue of his apostolic charge. But his principal concern is to justify and explain why he intends, after visiting Jerusalem, to abandon the field of his missionary work up till now (Asia Minor and Greece) and seek fresh harvest in the West. This future work in the Western Mediterranean, rather than the spiritual well-being of the Roman community, now seems to be uppermost in his mind. One could get the impression that Rome is to function as little more than a stopover on the way. Nonetheless, Paul wants to be "sped on his way" (v. 24) by the Romans. He seems to be enlisting their acceptance, their sympathy and perhaps their active support for his missionary work in the West. The letter would serve this aim by providing for the community a first-hand introduction to his gospel, necessary perhaps to counter distorted accounts of his character and mode of operation.

Beneath the tactful statements in these sections, however, one does pick up a subtle but unmistakable reminder that as apostle to the Gentiles Paul does have an obligation and duty with regard to the Romans, as they have to him. He has the right to see that all communities where there are Gentile as well as Jewish-Christians are properly conformed to the gospel, especially as regards relationships between both parties. This right extends even to communities not founded by himself. In view of this prerogative the practical instructions in chapters 12-15 are presumably no less relevant to the Roman community than the direct presentation of his gospel in chapters 1-11. Through the good effect of this letter Paul hopes to find in Rome a community well-disposed towards him and sympathetic to his mission — and one exhibiting in its relationships that conformity to the gospel he insisted upon in the communities founded by himself.

The choice between regarding Romans as a general treatise or seeing it directed to a particular situation may not in fact be as stark as once appeared. Recent studies of the literary form in which Paul's letters are cast have suggested that they fall into the category of "letter-essay," well-attested in the Mediterranean world.[1] As such Romans could well be addressed to a particular situation of which Paul had some knowledge, while at the same time constituting a summary of the teaching presupposed in his other letters and intended for a wider audience.

The Apocalyptic Background to Paul's Thought in Romans

Compared to earlier letters of Paul, notably 1 Thessalonians, but also 1 & 2 Corinthians, Romans seems at first glance to be remarkably lacking in features characteristic of "apocalyptic." Here I have in mind motifs such as the threat of an impending judgment, preceded by disaster and turmoil on a cosmic scale, the overthrow of spiritual powers hostile to God, detailed scenarios of the events of the end, including the resurrection of the dead: all described in rich and fantastic detail of imagery and language (cf. 1 Thess 4:13-18; 2 Thess 1:3 – 2:12; 1 Cor 15:51-57; 2 Cor 5:1-9; Mark 13 and the whole of Revelation). It is certainly the case that this later letter reflects a maturing of Paul's religious thought concerning the future. But, nonetheless, there is increasing recognition that Romans remains thoroughly "apocalyptic" in character and cannot be rightly interpreted except against this background.

---

[1] Cf. M.L. Stirewalt, Jr., "The Form and Function of the Greek Letter-Essay," in (K.P. Donfried ed.) *The Romans Debate*, (Minneapolis: Augsburg, 1977) pp. 175-206.

a) Jewish Apocalyptic

What are the chief features of apocalyptic? The word itself comes from the Greek for "uncovering" or "revelation." It refers to the way in which, after the close of prophetic activity in Israel, God was understood to be communicating with his people. This was through visions and heavenly transports granted to seers, who, usually at the behest of angels, recorded what they had seen and heard for the consolation and encouragement of the faithful. The Book of Daniel provides the only complete example of this kind of literature in the Old Testament — though apocalyptic traits are to be found in earlier literature, e.g., Isaiah 24-27; Ezekiel 38-39; Zechariah 12, 14. At the close of the Old Testament period, a time when the political and social fortunes of the nation had sunk to a notably low level, apocalyptic had come to be the dominant mode of Jewish religious sentiment and literary expression.

That Apocalyptic should flourish at such a time is understandable. For the apocalyptic cast of thinking tends to emerge out of a situation of great difficulty for the faithful community. It is marked by a strong sense of despair in human resources. It sees no hope for improvement arising out of social or political change on a human, this-worldly level. Only a dramatic, direct intervention of God himself can avail. The prophets of Israel had pointed out religious and social failure and indicated the disasters that would come to the people as a result. They saw the chastening — and ultimately salvific — hand of God operating on a this-worldly historical scale, employing the nations of this world and their rulers (e.g., Cyrus) as instruments. But for the apocalyptic writers the present, historical world is quite beyond redemption. They look to its total destruction and its replacement by another world newly-created by God.

In apocalyptic, then, there is a profound pessimism about the present world and its authorities, a pervasive sense of sin and a tendency to see everything in totally black and white terms. Outside the holy community (usually Israel, but often a restricted, faithful remnant within the wider faithless nation) all remains captive to evil spiritual forces, of which the oppressive Gentile rulers are tools. The faithful can only await the condemnation and ultimate destruction of these forces at the judgment that will accompany the intervention of God.

With this longed-for intervention at the end of time as its central focus the apocalyptic literature is naturally dominated by "eschatology," that is, concern for the events of the "end." Across the range of the literature there is considerable variation in the eschatological "program." In some cases a more this-worldly hope, characteristic of earlier Judaism, is retained, in others the hope is transmuted to a more transcendental, other-worldly level. But, nonetheless, a fairly constant pattern of expectation for the events of the end does emerge. In all cases there is a sharp division between this present age, characterized by sin and the triumph of evil and involving persecution and suffering for the faithful community, and the "age to come," the time of God's triumph and sovereignty, when the faithful will inherit all the blessings of the salvation promised to Israel.

Between the two eras and in some reports preceded by a period of evil even more rampant than that which prevails at present, stands the time of God's intervention. The climax of this will be the great judgment, where sentence will be passed upon the wicked, while the faithful stand vindicated or "justified" in the sight of their foes. Once maligned and accused of all manner of evil, they are now declared to be innocent, to have been in the right. It is in virtue of this "justification" pronounced by God that they will pass into the new age to enjoy the everlasting bliss of the kingdom of God.

Most depictions of this eschatological scenario in the apocalyptic literature assign a role to an angelic or quasi-angelic figure who becomes the *instrument of God's intervention.* In some cases such a figure appears to be little more than a passive symbol representative of the fate and ultimate triumph of the just. In others he takes an active role in the overthrow of the powers hostile to God and executes judgment himself. The installation of such a figure and his empowering with the Spirit for the accomplishment of his work marks the beginning of the events of the end.

In the mature period of the Jewish apocalyptic hope expectation of this angelic or transcendent figure seems to have blended with the older, more "this-worldly" hope for an ideal king of the lineage of David, who would re-establish in peace and righteousness the glories of the Davidic kingdom. In this way the messianic expectation of Israel took on the more transcendent, "other-worldly" features associated with the apocalyptic hope. The "Messiah" would be no merely human king, "anointed" to re-enact the glories of David's reign. He would be installed and empowered by the Spirit of God to play a key role in the downfall of the present (evil) world-order and the establishment on a cosmic scale of the rule or kingdom of God. To what extent the two conceptions of the expected one had already fused in the Jewish eschatology is not altogether clear. But certainly the earliest strands of Christianity show a blending of the two in the faith in Jesus of Nazareth as the Messiah.

Another feature of the apocalyptic eschatology that was to become a central tenet of Christian belief was the idea of "*resurrection*." As is well known, the idea of life after death is virtually absent from the Old Testament. Only towards the close of that period does it emerge in Jewish literature and then in two more or less distinct forms: 1. as "resurrection" in the apocalyptic literature, headed by the Book of Daniel (cf. 12:2); 2. as "immortality of the soul" in the literature more under the influence of Greek culture and ideas. In both cases the idea seems to be very much connected with the sense that the righteous dead, especially the martyrs who have given their lives in fidelity to the law and the Jewish faith, should not be denied a place in the final kingdom of God. In the apocalyptic literature, in particular, there is a strong link between the resurrection of the dead and the restoration of the Israel of the New Age. The apocalyptic scenario for the events of the end thus came to feature the resurrection of the dead as a key prelude to the

inauguration of the final kingdom, a once-for-all commu-
nal event to reconstitute a full and complete Israel. What
role the Messiah was to play in this is not clear. But certainly, as the transcendent and glorious instrument of God,
he does not die and so is not himself a candidate for
resurrection.

b) Christian Apocalyptic

The beginnings of the Christian faith lie entirely within the
framework of this apocalyptic Judaism. At the center of
Jesus' own preaching lay the proclamation that the "kingdom" or "rule" of God was imminent and the summons to
conversion of heart that its arrival required. He pointed to
his exorcisms, his miracles of healing and his teaching as
evidence that in his presence the "kingdom" had in some
sense already arrived (cf. Luke 1:20). After his death, the
core of the disciples' faith was the belief that the crucified
Jesus had been raised and exalted by God, established and
"anointed" in power to fulfil the role envisaged by apocalyptic Judaism for the Messiah. In lively hope they awaited his
imminent return in glory to execute judgment and complete
the establishment of the Kingdom of God.

But this Christian application of the apocalyptic hope to
Jesus of Nazareth involved some drastic revisions to the
standard eschatological program of apocalyptic Judaism.
That program, as we have seen, never had to cater for a
Messiah who died and entered upon his messianic rule via
resurrection. Nor, in its resurrection hope did it envisage any
kind of time-gap between the resurrection of one key figure
(the Messiah) and the raising of the rest. To acknowledge
Jesus as the Messiah, however, meant understanding the
intervention of God as occurring in a far more complex way:
first, the preaching of the earthly Jesus as a summons to
conversion before the coming of the kingdom; then the
death of Jesus, understood as a sacrifice atoning for sin; his
resurrection, seen as the inauguration of God's judgment
and final sovereignty but not as its completion. The "end"
would come only after a period wholly uncatered for in the

Jewish eschatology — what later came to be seen as the "time of the Church." This is the time between the resurrection of Jesus, and his final coming in glory, the time when his messianic work continues through the Spirit.

In the early post-Easter period Christians coped with the problem created by this (unforeseen) "gap" by supposing that it would be of very short duration. It gave a space for a wider preaching of the gospel of repentance — first to Jews and later Gentiles.

But as the years went by and Jesus did not return, dealing with the problem created by this time-gap seems to have become a major preoccupation of early Christian reflection. We find its imprint upon virtually all the New Testament documents, as in various ways and in varying degrees they attempt to find theological meaning and value in the present interim existence, its institutions and its structures. All this marked a significant shift away from the more rigorous time scheme of the earlier apocalyptic eschatology. It was accelerated by the process whereby Christianity became less and less bound to its Jewish origins and came to be proclaimed in forms and language more acceptable to the wider Mediterranean world, where more static, less apocalyptic views of salvation were favoured.

Across the span of Paul's writings we can observe this shift in eschatology. In an early letter such as 1 Thessalonians the apocalyptic perspective and temper is very marked. In Romans, as we shall see, the tone is less strident, the imagery more restrained. But apocalyptic remains central to the language, the content and the argument as a whole. The Paul of Romans is still very much bound up with the basic Christian problem of asserting over against Judaism a more complex and more subtle eschatology. For God has shattered the expected "program," upset the neat division of "present age" and "age to come." In Christ he has initiated the final relationship with himself and given the Spirit as its pledge. But he has not yet done away completely with the present evil time. God has in this sense broken all the "eschatological rules." The debate in Romans reflects this problem on almost every page.

The Structure of Romans

Confining ourselves to Romans 1-15, we will note *Intro-ductory* and *Concluding* sections 1:1-15 and 15:14-33. These two passages, which we have considered in connection with the purpose and occasion of the letter, constitute its outer "frames." They hold the intervening sections together as a pair of bookends contain volumes on a shelf. Immediately following the introduction comes a solemn statement of the *Theme* of the letter: 1:16-17. These two verses introduce within their brief compass much of the key theological language of Paul.

The *Body* of the letter then begins at 1:18 and continues down to 15:13. According to the general pattern of Paul's letters, it falls into two parts: 1. a section devoted principally to a statement of the gospel (*kerygma*); 2. a statement more concerned with the gospel's application to Christian life (*didachê*).

As we have already noted, in Romans the first, kerygmatic section is of disproportionately great length, running from 1:18 to the end of chap. 11 (11:36). It contains three major parts: 1. In the first, 1:18 - 4:25, Paul establishes his basic principle that the eschatological justification is available for all, Jews and Gentiles alike, solely on the basis of *faith,* not on performance of the law. Within this section, he first establishes the universal need for such a justification (1:18 - 3:20). In a solemn statement taking up the original theme, he then proclaims its availability through the revelation of God's righteousness in Christ (3:21-31). The argument of this section is then clinched by adducing Abraham as Scripture's proof that God justifies and grants salvation on the basis of faith alone (4:1-25). 2. The chapter on Abraham acts as something of a bridge to the second major section, 5:1 - 8:39, where the principal theme is that of *hope* — hope of obtaining the eschatological blessings of salvation on the basis of the right-standing with God obtained through faith. In the middle of this section, 6:1 - 8:13, there is, as I shall argue, a long *"Ethical Excursus"* devoted to the possibility and the necessity of living-out the righteousness obtained by grace.

The latter part of chap. 8 (8:14-39) resumes the thought of chap. 5, asserting the sure hope of salvation through the victory of God's love. ③ The third section, chaps. 9-11, at first sight the most "detachable" part of Romans, is wholly devoted to the immense problem created by the failure of the bulk of Israel to come to faith in Jesus as the Christ. A short hymn to God's unsearchable wisdom, 11:33-36, brings this lengthy kerygmatic part of Romans to a close.

The "applied" section of Romans, 12:1 - 15:13, is chiefly concerned to commend right relationships within the Christian community. Chap. 12 treats of unity in a fairly general way and this continues through chap. 13, save for a notable section, 13:1-7, where relationship with civil authorities is discussed. Chaps 14 and 15:1-13, as we have noted, treat of unity and tolerance in the more specific context of food and drink. Chap. 16, which we shall not consider, consists chiefly of personal greetings sent by Paul to members of the community.[2]

[2] There is some textual evidence casting doubt upon the inclusion of chap. 16 in the original letter to Rome. For a helpful discussion of this question see Robinson, *Wrestling with Romans* pp. 2-5.

Structure of Romans 1-15: Outline

INTRODUCTION:
    1:1-15: Address, Greeting, Thanksgiving
THEME:
    1:16-17: Good News of Salvation
            through the Saving Justice of God
BODY OF LETTER:
    1:18 - 15:33

I. 1:18 - 11:36:
    Exposition of the Gospel (Kerygma)

    A: 1:18 – 4:25:
        Justification on the basis of Faith

            i. 1:18 - 3:20:
                The Universal Need for God's Justice

                    a) 1:18-32: Gentile World
                    b) 2:1-16: Jewish World (1)
                    c) 2:17-29: Jewish World (2)
                    d) 3:1-20: Universal Sinfulness

            ii. 3:21-31: The Revelation of
                            God's Saving Justice in Christ

            iii. 4:1-25:   Abraham as Faith Person
                            and Bearer of the Promise

    B: 5:1 – 8:39: The new basis for Hope

            i. 5:1-11: Hope of Glory in the face of Suffering

            ii. 5:12-21: Solidarity in Christ stronger than
                            Solidarity in Adam

            iii. 6:1 - 8:13: "Ethical Excursus"

READING:

Purpose & Occasion:
The most useful documents on this question are gathered
together in K.P. Donfried (ed.), *The Romans Debate*
(Minneapolis: Augsburg, 1977)
— see especially the articles by Manson, Bornkamm,
Donfried, Karris and Stirewalt.
The following survey articles by W. S. Campbell should
now be added:
"The Romans Debate," *Journal for the Study of the
New Testament* 10 (1981) 19-28;
"Revisiting Romans," *Scripture Bulletin* 12 (1981) 2-10.

Apocalyptic Background:
J.C. Beker, *Paul the Apostle* (Philadelphia: Fortress, 1980)
135-52.

*J.J. Collins, *The Apocalyptic Imagination: An Introduc-
tion to the Jewish Matrix of Christianity* (New York:
Crossroad) 1-32.

P.D. Hanson, *The Dawn of Apocalyptic* (2nd ed., Philadelphia: Fortress, 1979) 1-31.

K. Koch, *The Rediscovery of Apocalyptic* (Napierville:
Allenson, 1972).

N. Perrin and D.C. Duling, *The New Testament: An Introduction* (2nd ed.; New York: Harcourt Brace Jovanovich,
1982) 27-30, 96-99, 480-81.

*D.S. Russell, *The Method and Message of Jewish Apoca-
lyptic* (London: SCM, 1964; Philadelphia: Westminster).

1

Paul, the Servant of the Gospel
1:1-15

Address

¹Paul, a servant of Jesus Christ, called to be an apostle, set apart for the gospel of God, ²which he announced before-hand, through his prophets in the holy scriptures, ³the gospel concerning his Son,

> who was born of the seed of David according to the flesh,
> ⁴who was designated Son of God in power according to the spirit of holiness, from the time of his resurrection from the dead,
>
> Jesus Christ, our Lord.

⁵Through him we have received grace and our apostolic mission to bring about the obedience of faith for the honor of his name amongst all the nations, ⁶including yourselves, who are called to belong to Jesus Christ. ⁷ᵃTo all of you, then, in Rome, beloved of God and called to be saints:

Greeting

⁷ᵇGrace to you and peace from God our Father and the Lord Jesus Christ.

Thanksgiving

[8]First of all, I give thanks to my God through Jesus Christ for all of you, because all over the world they tell of your faith. [9]For God is my witness, the God whom I serve with all my spirit preaching the gospel of his Son: how unfailingly I make mention of you in my prayers, [10]always asking that somehow at long last I may, through his will, succeed in coming to visit you. [11]For I long to see you in order to impart some spiritual gift for your strengthening, [12]that is, that we may be mutually encouraged by our common faith, yours and mine. [13]I want you to know, brothers, that I have often planned to come to you — but until now have always been prevented — in order to reap some harvest among you as among the rest of the Gentiles. [14]For I am under obligation both to Greeks and non-Greeks, to the educated and uneducated alike. [15]That is why I am eager to preach the gospel to you also who are in Rome.

Paul begins his letter to the Romans with his own standard modification of the "letter-essay" opening: an Address (1:1-7a), a Greeting (1:7b) and a Thanksgiving (1:8-15). The third element, though technically a prayer of gratitude to God for the graces bestowed upon the community, allows Paul tactfully to compliment the community, while also hinting at his own plans and agenda. We have already considered these verses in some detail when discussing the occasion and purpose of the letter. Here we shall confine our remarks to certain elements of the Address, in particular to Paul's statement about "gospel" in vv. 3-4.

Writing to commend himself to a community which he had not personally founded, Paul introduces himself to the Romans in terms of more than usual formality. The title "servant of Jesus Christ" evokes the scriptural designation of prophets as "servants" of God. "Set apart for the gospel of God" continues this link, echoing the call of the prophet Jeremiah (Jer 1:5). The apostles re-enact both the calling and the proclamation of the prophets. Where the prophets discerned and proclaimed the intervention of God in human history, the apostles proclaim the message of the culminating, eschatological intervention of God — a message itself foreshadowed and "pre-announced" in the prophetic writings (v. 2).

In vv. 3-4 Paul gives what virtually amounts to a "definition" of the gospel. Before considering it we need to spend some time trying to catch the precise resonances of "gospel" in his understanding. Since from beginning to end Romans is nothing more or less than a complete statement of Paul's gospel, an excursion into the background of the term needs no apology.

Gospel

In the Pauline literature the Greek noun "gospel" (*euaggelion*) and the cognate verb "to preach" (*euaggelizein*) enjoy a prominence unparalleled in the rest of the New Testament. (The verb is frequent in Luke and Acts, but absent in Matthew and Mark. The noun occurs occasionally in Matthew, Mark and Acts, but not in the gospel of Luke. Both noun and verb are absent from the Johannine literature). From this one might suspect that the whole idea of "gospel" is a peculiarly Pauline one. However, there are good grounds for believing that behind Paul's usage stretched a rich tradition concerning "gospel."

In the Greek version of the Old Testament (Septuagint) the wordgroup *euaggelion/euaggelizein* was used to translate the Hebrew stem *bśr*, which has the meaning "tell good news." In the early literature the verbal form *mbśr* occurs with some frequency in the general sense of telling good news after, e.g., victory in battle (cf. 1 Sam 31:9). Later on, *mbśr* appears in a more precise context where the "good news" has to do with the breaking-in of God's rule and the coming of his salvation. This development can already be seen in Pss 40:9 and 96:2. But in a cluster of passages in Isaiah 40-66 (40:9; 41:27; 52:7; 60:6; 61:1; cf. Nah 1:15) *mbśr* becomes virtually a technical term for the announcement of the salvation proclaimed by the prophet. Here *mbśr* is linked to themes such as freedom from bondage, the rule or kingship of Yahweh, the coming era of salvation, peace and righteousness, the "anointing" of the messenger with the Spirit, a return to Jerusalem accompanied by transformation of the wilderness and other miracles of healing and peace.

This "good news" theme of Isaiah 40-66 had as its primary focus the end of the Babylonian captivity and exile. There is evidence, however, that the quasi-technical sense of "tell the good news" derived from Isaiah was preserved in the Jewish tradition to be applied to the hope for salvation in the more apocalyptic sense characteristic of the later period. The most striking evidence for this comes from the so-called "Melchisedek Scroll" from Qumran Cave 11. In this (very fragmentary) text two of the Isaiah passages, 52:7 and 61:1, are linked precisely via the "good news" motif. The "good news" is proclaimed by one "anointed with the Spirit" and concerns the eschatological liberation of the holy community from the dominion of evil powers through the agency of a heavenly being, who seems to be the archangel Michael. In the context of God's "kingdom" or "rule" being established, Michael functions as the eschatological High Priest, making atonement for sin in the last and final Day of Atonement and so opening the way to eternal life. Here the key ideas that attach to "gospel" in Isaiah 40-66 are given a stronger eschatological note and joined to the sense of the need for freedom from sin characteristic of apocalyptic Judaism.

It should be clear that in such a text we are coming very close to the ideas that attach to "gospel" in the New Testament. One is particularly reminded of the opening words of Jesus in the Gospel of Mark: "The time is fulfilled and the kingdom of God is at hand; repent and believe in the gospel" (1:15). This impression is reinforced when we recall that the one who makes this announcement is the one who has just been "anointed with the Spirit" after his baptism (1:10-11) and who now goes on to carry out a ministry of "exorcism," that is, of liberating human beings from the grip of evil spirits (cf. 1:21-28, 32-34; also Luke 4:16-44; Acts 10:36, 38, 42).

Just how early and how widely in early Christian circles the proclamation of Jesus came to be made in "good news/gospel" terms is not altogether clear. Besides the tradition flowing from the Old Testament, the use of *euaggelion* in secular Greek to announce the "good news" of the emperor's arrival or birthday undoubtedly made a contribution. Paul, at any rate, writing to a community at Rome that he had not himself evangelized, can presuppose "gospel" to be part of the accepted technical language of the Christian churches. And that his own use of "gospel" sat closely to the Isaianic background is clear from its close association in his thought with themes such as "righteousness," "salvation," etc., also characteristic of Isaiah 40-66.

So, while the evidence is not conclusive, there are good grounds for believing that the early Christian community or at least important sectors of it took over from apocalyptic Judaism the tradition of applying the "good news" language of Isaiah 40-66 to the coming intervention of God. In the preaching of Jesus himself, as presented in the Synoptic tradition, the central focus of the gospel lies upon the proclamation of the kingdom of God (cf. Mark 1:15, quoted above). In the preaching of the community after the death of Jesus the focus has shifted and come to rest upon Jesus himself. In the words of the famous dictum, "The Proclaimer has become the Proclaimed." The gospel is now "about" Jesus Christ. This does not mean an abandonment of the wider eschatological perspective; the "kingdom of God" remains the ultimate hope. But it does mean recognition that Jesus of Nazareth, crucified and raised from the dead, is the "anointed" agent of God, the chosen instrument according to the expectations of apocalyptic Judaism for the ushering in of the kingdom. If God has set up Jesus as Messiah, he has finally and irrevocably set in motion the events of the end. The "good news" about Jesus, then, is at one and the same time the "good news" about the imminence of the kingdom of God.

Paul's "Definition" of the Gospel (1:3-4)

Returning now to the text of Romans 1, we can safely assume that Paul's use of "gospel" lies within this apocalyptic framework and expectation. By "gospel" he means the announcement that God has at last set in motion the eschatological events leading to the judgment, the salvation of the elect and the establishment of God's rule. This "gospel of

God" (v. 1) was "proclaimed beforehand by the prophets in
the holy scriptures" (v. 2) — presumably Isaiah 40-66 is in
view. It is now "the gospel concerning his Son" (v. 3) because
the setting up of Jesus as the messianic agent of God is the
key event inaugurating the eschatological process. Hence the
statement contained in vv. 3-4 constitutes a summary of the
gospel in the sense that it describes the setting-up of Jesus in
this role of Messiah.

It is generally agreed that in vv. 3-4 Paul is quoting an
early credal summary of the gospel. The most basic indication of this comes from the formal symmetry of the
statement:

> "Concerning his Son,
>> who was born of the Seed of David according to the flesh,
>> who was designated Son of God in power according to the
>> spirit of holiness from the time of his resurrection from
>> the dead,
> Jesus Christ, our Lord.

It is hard to catch the symmetry of the Greek participial
construction in translation. But the total statement clearly
refers in sequence to two distinct stages of what might be
termed the "career" of Jesus Christ. On the level of purely
human descent he was born of the "Seed of David." That is,
in terms of his human origins Jesus fulfilled the key messianic credential of belonging to the royal house of David and
was in this sense a "candidate" Messiah. The parallel statement refers to Jesus' existence in the order of the "Spirit,"
that is, from the perspective of the creative, transforming
power which both accompanies and signifies God's eschatological intervention into the world. In this order, of which
the resurrection of Jesus is the first moment, the "candidate"
Messiah has been installed as "Son of God" in power. He is
now Messiah in fact, clad with the power of the Spirit for the
carrying out of God's eschatological plan.

In terms of the original formula Jesus is constituted Son
of God "from the time of his resurrection from the dead."

This could suggest an "adoptionist" christology according to which Jesus only becomes "Son" at the resurrection. But the title "Son of God" here in this early formula hardly carries the full christological loading it was later to acquire — in the Gospel of John, for instance and subsequent Christian literature. It is rather a title the Jewish tradition applied to God's Anointed without any suggestion of an essential filial relationship to God. What the formula basically states is that Jesus, who in the order of his human origins fulfilled the Davidic credentials for being Messiah, has been at his resurrection solemnly installed as Messiah, which means that God has inaugurated the events of the end, the New Age of the Spirit.

Paul's own understanding of Jesus, as is clear from several other passages (cf. Rom 8:3-4, 32; Gal 4:4-5), goes deeper than this. For him Jesus is "Son" already during his earthly life (and possibly also in a "pre-existent" state: cf. Phil 2:6; 2 Cor 8:9). It is probably in view of this fuller understanding that he introduces into the formula the phrase "in power," which otherwise disturbs the symmetry. For Paul it was not the resurrection which made Jesus God's Son. He had enjoyed that dignity, albeit in a hidden way, throughout his earthly life. The resurrection meant the public revelation of that status, the unveiling of the true identity of Jesus and of his function within the eschatological plan of God. It is this that the gospel proclaims.

Following his quotation of the formula of faith, Paul (v. 5) indicates his own distinct role in this "economy" of salvation. From the Risen Lord he has received the "grace of apostleship," with the distinct charge to bring about an "obedience of faith" among the Gentiles. What does this evocative phrase mean? In the first place, it suggests a close association in Paul's mind between "obedience" and "faith." More precisely in this context, Paul is probably hinting that, just as the Israel of old was virtually defined as the "obedient nation," practicing an obedience of fidelity to the law, so now he has been charged to gather from all nations a final People of God, defined solely on the basis of that obedience which stems from faith.

READING:

"Gospel":

J.A. Fitzmyer, "The Gospel in the Theology of Paul," in *To Advance the Gospel* (New York: Crossroad, 1981) 149-61; originally in *Interpretation* 33 (1979) 339-50.

G. Friedrich, Art. *"euaggelizomai, euaggelion,...,"* in (G. Kittel ed.) *Theological Dictionary of the New Testament,* 2.707-37.

O. Piper, Art. "Gospel (Message)," in *Interpreter's Dictionary of the Bible,* 2.442-48.

P. Stuhlmacher, *Das paulinische Evangelium* I. *Vorgeschichte* (Göttingen: Vandenhoeck & Ruprecht, 1968).

Rom 1:3-4:

B.J. Byrne, *'Sons of God' — 'Seed of Abraham'* (Rome: Biblical Institute, 1979) 205-11.

J.D.G. Dunn, "Jesus Flesh and Spirit: An Exegesis of Romans I.3-4," *Journal of Theological Studies* NS 24 (1973) 40-68.

*M. Hengel, *The Son of God* (Philadelphia: Fortress, 1976; London: SCM) 59-66.

2

The Gospel of God's Saving Justice
1:16-17

Theme

[16]For I am not ashamed of the gospel — It is the power of God leading to salvation for everyone who has faith, the Jew first, but also the Greek. [17]For in it the righteousness of God is being revealed, from faith to faith, as it is written: *The person who is right with God through faith will live* (Hab 2:4).

In this statement Paul formally announces the theme of his letter to Rome. The statement also introduces the key terms and concepts in which his message is to be cast. Our consideration of this passage will chiefly consist in pursuing the meaning of these terms in the Jewish apocalyptic background which Paul both presupposes and challenges in Romans.

"Gospel" we have already considered. It is the solemn announcement that at last the key events leading up to God's eschatological intervention have been set in train. Paul here makes clear that he does not regard the gospel simply as a message, an announcement. When received with faith and allowed to grasp one's being it becomes a transforming power, setting one creatively within the unfolding pattern of those events leading to salvation.

Salvation: Fullness of Humanity

But what does Paul mean by "*salvation*?" Setting aside the theological overlay of the centuries, let us explore his understanding within the apocalyptic framework. If we keep in mind the "program" envisaged in that framework, "salvation," in the first place and negatively, means rescue, liberation from the captivity of the present (evil) age. Positively, it means entrance into the new age and the obtaining of the eschatological blessings promised to the faithful.

This may sound remote and even "alienating" to modern ears. However, as further study of Romans will show, the eschatological blessings, for all their fanciful depiction in some apocalyptic literature, were not seen as a "pie in the sky." In essence they constitute the fulfilment of God's original and still valid design for human beings as outlined in Genesis 1-3: the achievement of true humanity, within the context of due relationship to God and a constructive attitude to the non-human world.

The complete attainment of such salvation remains in the future. But, in a way scarcely envisaged in the Jewish apocalyptic framework, Paul begins to feel his way towards a foreshadowing of salvation here and now. In the renewed relationship with God brought about through faith the barrier between the "present age" and the "age to come" begins to crumble. Salvation begins here and now when men and women in the power of the Spirit achieve a deeper humanity and become themselves agents of wider humanization. That such is Paul's idea of "salvation" remains to be shown from the text of Romans. But even on the basis of what he is presupposing, a definition of "salvation" in terms of true humanity is not premature.

Faith

Paul in v. 16 says the gospel is the power of God leading to salvation for "every believer." Here we must keep in mind that in Greek the verb "believe" (*pisteuein*) and the noun "faith" (*pistis*) are cognate and so echo one another with a resonance impossible to convey in English. The full meaning of *"faith/believe"* can only emerge as the argument of Romans unfolds (By the end of chap. 4 at least three further elements will have to be included). But for the present and provisionally let us offer the following. In the first place and following an Old Testament tradition, Paul understands faith as involving both an attitude and a personal commitment. It is that attitude which discerns God acting creatively in the world and in one's life and which surrenders to that claim in confidence and trust. The opposite of idolatry, faith responds to God precisely as Creator and allows that response centrally and exclusively to determine life.

Paul says *"every* believer." With this single word "every" (expanded later as "the Jew first, but also the Greek") he catches up a central theme of the letter: the universal scope of the gospel and the salvation it proclaims. He speaks positively but there is already here a subtle polemic. The "inclusiveness" of the gospel in that it requires simply faith excludes its restriction to a single nation claiming unique credentials: possession of the law of Moses.

What is at stake here is not simply the law but a whole religious attitude Paul sees going with it. That is an attitude which, primarily concerned for individual salvation and well-being, attempts to win God's favor through personal moral achievement. Over against this, Paul's intention in Romans is to establish that what comes first is a response in faith to God's offer of relationship. The moral life of individuals involves nothing more or less than the living out of that relationship with God, which includes being "built into" his creative responsibility for the world.

The Righteousness of God: Saving Justice

Mention of God's creative responsibility for the world leads us to the phrase of most central importance in Paul's statement of theme: the "righteousness of God" (*hê dikaiosunê tou theou*). Here, above all, it is important to go back behind centuries of controversy in an attempt to grasp Paul's own understanding. The Greek word *dikaiosunê*, was translated into Latin as *iustitia*. This Latin usage lies behind the English translation "justice" customary in the Catholic tradition. The Reformation tradition, on the other hand, has favored "righteousness."

Neither translation has served Paul well. "Justice" in common parlance has the sense of "impartiality," "fairness" — especially in bestowing rewards and punishments. Such an understanding of "justice of God," reinforced by an uninformed understanding of "the anger of God" in v. 18, can make and has made for a singularly grim and unfortunate interpretation of Paul's redemption statement in 3:21-26. "Righteousness" is perhaps less loaded and more restricted to theological usage. But this restriction is at once both strength and weakness. It tends to be understood in a narrowly individualistic way, whereas "justice," for all its unfortunate overtones, at least hints at wider, social implications. For the sake of clarity I shall retain the translation "righteousness" when commenting on the text. But it is vital to keep in mind the nuances of "fidelity" and "saving justice" which attach to the term in the biblical tradition Paul presupposes. This background we must now examine in some detail.

The Righteousness of God: The Jewish Background

The word *dikaiosunê* is used in the Greek version of the Old Testament (the Septuagint) to translate a variety of Hebrew terms. But overwhelmingly it translates the Hebrew word group *ṣedeq/ṣedaqah*. This word group appears to

7

7

have a basic association with the Ancient Near Eastern concept of cosmic and/or social order. The essential idea in *ṣedeq/ṣedaqah* is fidelity — and fidelity precisely within the pattern of relationships that guarantee, preserve and enhance the cosmic and social order.

Ṣedaqah is often defined, then, as "fidelity within the demands of a relationship." It refers, however, not so much to an attribute of a person but to action. Action or behavior is designated as "righteous" or done "in righteousness" when it accords with the upholding of the relationship and the right order that depends upon it. Persons are "righteous" not so much when they are moral in a general kind of way, but when they act in accord with the demands of a relationship, when they "do the right thing by someone." The classic biblical illustration is the acknowledgment given by Judah with respect to Tamar in Gen 38:26: "She is more righteous than I."

In the Israelite understanding cosmic and social order was seen as determined in all spheres through the relationship with *God*. This relationship ("covenant" being its key expression) and the "righteousness" that went with it underpinned the national life and the entire social order. In his "righteousness" Yahweh creates and nourishes the life of his people: giving growth and fertility through the cycle of the seasons, giving victory and rescue to his people in time of war (saving acts), ensuring proper social order through the setting up and guidance of key officials (the king, judges, etc.). There is a real continuity between the righteousness shown by Yahweh in his activity as Creator and that of his saving acts on behalf of the people: Pss 67; 97; 98; 111; 145; 147; Isaiah 41; 45-46; 48:12-19; 51:1-13; 54; 61-62). Righteousness flows out from Yahweh as from a source of power. As Creator, savior and guarantor of the social order, he is hymned for his righteousness in the cultic life of the nation (cf. esp. Pss 47; 93; 95-99).

On the *human* side a corresponding righteousness is required. This righteousness is operative with respect both to God and to fellow human beings. But in fact there is a real continuity. Prosperity and good social order (*shalom*) depend on the extent to which the key figures (the king, judges, etc.) and indeed all Israelites share and reflect in their lives the righteousness emanating from Yahweh (Pss 18; 72; 82; 101). Cut off from this creative source, their actions become perverted and the social fabric breaks down (Amos 5:25; 6:12; Isaiah 58; Ps 82). When this breakdown occurs, wronged individuals can appeal to the "God of justice" (Pss 5; 7; 22; 31; 58; 71; 140; 143).

"Deeds of righteousness" can apply to just government, ethical uprightness in personal and social life, truthfulness, gracious and generous activity reflecting Yahweh's own kindness. But "righteousness" does not refer simply to virtue in general. Essentially it designates what makes for and preserves the relationships upon which the social and religious fabric of the people is built. Righteousness means participating in the responsibility of the Creator towards Israel and the entire created world.

A particular locus for "righteousness" is the *law-court* situation. Hence the concept of "forensic" righteousness. In a law-court persons are "put in the right" ("justified," "rightwised") when declared innocent and acquitted, when their behavior is declared to have been in conformity with community standards. "Justification" lifts the stigma of accusation which put in question their relationship with the community. It restores them to full relationship.

The situation of the Exile (the "Babylonian Captivity") caused the *saving* and *eschatological* aspects of God's righteousness to come to the fore. In certain Psalms (e.g., 96, 98) and in Isaiah 40-66 in particular, *sedaqah* characterizes God"s gracious, saving acts on behalf of his (captive) people. It becomes virtually a technical term expressing his "saving fidelity" (over 50 occurrences). In many cases *sedaqah* stands for the result of such saving activity, becoming synonymous with "*salvation*," "deliverance" (Is 45:8; 46:12-13; 51:5-6), "restoration of national life" (43:16-21), "peace," "prosperity" and "glory." In this context, too, God's righteousness takes on three further aspects: 1. the eschatological — *sedaqah* is the coming salvation which God will bring to his people; 2. the forensic (law-court) —

Isaiah portrays God in process with his people (41:1, 21) or (more usually) with foreign nations and their gods (50:7-9); 3. the universal —the coming *sedaqah* touches not only the restoration of Israel but envisages Yahweh's sovereignty over all nations (Is 45:21-25; 49:6-7; 51:4-5; cf. Ps 96:10-13).

Frequently in the biblical tradition the acknowledgment of God's righteousness accompanies the confession of failure, of *un*righteousness on the part of *human beings* (e.g., Is 5:15-16; Ps 51:4l; 65:1-5; 143; Lam 1:18; Dan 9:13-19; Neh 9:33; 2 Chr 12:16). There is acknowledgment that God is in the right and Israel in the wrong and that the evils that have come are due to that lack of righteousness. God's righteousness here has a cleansing, purifying function with respect to sin. Whether in such connections it ever has a strictly punitive or destructive aspect is arguable (Is 10:22 is hardly certain evidence for this). God's righteousness works ultimately for healing and restoration of the life-giving relationship — even if this renewal is sometimes achieved through allowing Israel to suffer for a time the consequences of alienation (cf. Is 40:1-2; Jer 30:10-17).

Thus Israel, while acknowledging her own unrighteousness and fully accepting responsibility for the sufferings it has brought, knows that in her sinfulness and plight she can call with confidence precisely upon God's righteousness for rescue. Psalm 143 is the outstanding illustration of this:

> [1]Hear my prayer, O Lord; give ear to my entreaties.
> Answer me in your faithfulness, in your righteousness (*sedaqah*).
> [2]Enter not into judgment with your servant, for no one living is righteous before you.

[Vv. 3-10 describe the plight of the psalmist and beg for rescue]

> [11]For the sake of your name, O Lord, preserve my life. And in your righteousness (*sedaqah*) save me from trouble.

¹²And in your steadfast love cut off my enemies, for I am your servant.

The psalmist confesses his sinfulness and avers that no one is righteous in God's sight (v. 2). But he both begins (v. 1) and concludes (v. 11) his prayer with an appeal for rescue precisely to God in his righteousness. The psalmist is confident that, even though he has not been faithful to God, God remains faithful to him.

The *apocalyptic writings of late-Judaism* continue the "righteousness" tradition of Isaiah 40-66, but with ever greater stress upon the eschatological and forensic aspects and, in particular, with the dualistic sharpness characteristic of apocalyptic. There is increasing despair and pessimism about the possibility of any righteousness on the human side, save in the small community of the elect, whose righteousness is more and more seen to consist in faithful practice of the Law. Outside the chosen few, all is unrighteousness: the faithful can only wait upon the eschatological intervention of God. This exercise of his righteousness will mean freedom, vindication (sc. "justification") and the blessings of salvation for the righteous, but judgment, punishment for all besides (cf. Jub. 1:15; 21:4; 22:15; 31:25; 1 Enoch 71:3; 99:10; T. Dan. 6:10; 4 Ezra 8:20-26).

Within the same apocalyptic perspective, the *Scrolls from Qumran* feature a distinctive development of the Old Testament tradition of God's righteousness vis-à-vis human unrighteousness. In a context of confessing sin, the Qumran psalmist invokes the righteousness of God as the eschatological saving power, which here and now and as an expression of grace works cleansing, justification and renewal (1QS [*Community Rule*] XI: 2, 5, 12-14; 1QH [*Thanksgiving Psalms*] IV:36). *Other strands of Judaism,* notably the Pharisaic, tended increasingly to drive a wedge between God's righteousness and his mercy. God's righteousness is seen more in the category of a judicial uprightousness that rewards righteous deeds (especially the keeping of the law: "law-righteousness") and punishes offenses (Pss. Sol. 8:23-25; 9) Likewise, in the Greek-speaking world of Hellenistic Judaism the "saving" sense of *dikaiosunê* tended to give way to the sense of legal justice (cf. Wis 12:15).

The Righteousness of God: Paul

As our reading of Romans will show, *Paul's* idea of the "righteousness of God" harks back to the Old Testament tradition. He is particularly close to Isaiah 40-66, but shares also the eschatological sharpening and dualism characteristic of apocalyptic. With respect to the problem of sin, Paul stands closest to Qumran. But his exclusion of law-righteousness is unparalleled there — as is also his idea of a "justification" worked through faith in the atoning death of Christ, something which opens up salvation beyond the small elect community to embrace the whole world. For Paul God's righteousness consists in his saving fidelity as Creator to the entire creation, a fidelity exercised finally (that is, eschatologically) and universally in the redemptive work of God in Christ.

Recognizing this broad Old Testament-Apocalyptic background to Paul's idea of righteousness lifts the interpretation of Romans out of the entrenched view that it is concerned primarily with the justification of the individual before God. *Dikaiosunê* brings with it the whole pattern linking relationship with God intrinsically to the concern for right social order that attends *ṣedeq/ṣedaqah* in the Israelite theology. "Righteousness" is concerned with relationship — with the relationship to God in the first place, but also with that web of relationships between human beings and human groups essential for the enhancement of dignity and well-being. For this reason the understanding of God's righteousness as "saving justice," though inadequate, is appropriate. The main thing, however, when reading Romans is to escape the narrowness of single terms and keep in mind the broad and rich tradition presupposed by Paul.

For Paul the gospel is the "power of God leading to salvation" precisely because it gathers up believers into the scope of this "saving justice." He concludes this statement of theme in v. 17 with an enigmatic phrase, "from faith to faith," clinched by an equally enigmatic quotation from Hab 2:4: "The person who is right with God through faith will live." Interpretations here are legion. Paul has chosen not to specify "faith" too closely. This leaves open the possibility that "faith" can embrace both God's fidelity to his world and the human response in faith and trust. In particular, the fact that Paul omits possessive pronouns attaching to the Habakkuk quotation in the ancient versions (Hebrew: "The righteous person will live by his faith;" Greek: "The righteous person will live by my [i.e., God's] faithfulness") leaves the text open to a "messianic" sense, in which the primary reference would be to Christ. In his death and resurrection Jesus embodies both the faithful response of the just person in the face of evil and the fidelity of God bringing life out of death. For the present this is but a hint, a possibility. For explicit presentation of Christ as the embodiment of God's saving justice we must wait till chap. 3.

READING:

*M.T. Brauch, "Perspectives on 'God's Righteousness' in recent German discussion," in E.P. Sanders, *Paul and Palestinian Judaism* (Philadelphia: Fortress, 1977) 523-42.

*R. Bultmann, *Theology of the New Testament* (2 vols.; London: SCM, 1952, 1955) 1.270-79 ("Righteousness"), 314-21 ("Faith").

*E. Käsemann, "'The Righteousness of God' in Paul," in *New Testament Questions of Today* (Philadelphia: Fortress, 1969) 168-82.

*G. Klein, "Righteousness in the New Testament," in *The Interpreter's Dictionary of the Bible, Supplementary Volume,* 750-52.

*J. Reumann, *"Righteousness" in the New Testament,* (Philadelphia/New York: Fortress/Paulist, 1982) 12-22 (Old Testament Background), 64-91 (Romans).

S.K. Williams, "The 'Righteousness of God' in Romans," *Journal of Biblical Literature* 99 (1980) 241-90.

J.A. Ziesler, *The Meaning of Righteousness in Paul* (Cambridge: Cambridge University, 1972).

"Righteousness of God" — *Old Testament:*

K. Koch, Art. "ṣdq", *Theologisches Handwörterbuch zum Alten Testament* (Munich: Kaiser, 1976) 2. Cols. 507-30.

H. Graf Reventlow, *Rechtfertigung im Horizont des Alten Testaments,* Munich: Kaiser, 1971.

H.H. Schmid, *Gerechtigkeit als Weltordnung,* Tübingen: Mohr (Siebeck), 1968.

—————, "Rechtfertigung als Schöpfungsgeschehen: Notizen zum alttestamentlichen Vorgeschichte eines neutestamentlichen Themas," in (J. Friedrich et al. edd.) *Rechtfertigung: Festschrift für E. Käsemann zum 70. Geburtstag* (Tübingen/Göttingen: Mohr (Siebeck)/Vandenhoeck & Ruprecht, 1976) 403-14.

G. von Rad, *Old Testament Theology* (2 Vols., New York: Harper & Row, 1962, 1965; Edinburgh and London: Oliver & Boyd) 1.370-83.

3

The World's Need for
God's Justice (I): Gentiles
1:18-32

At this point we are poised to enter what is in many ways the most forbidding and least attractive part of Romans. All appears to be sin, wrath, and menace, as Paul catalogues the failure, first of the Gentile (1:18-32) and then the Jewish world (2:1-3:20). This was not, however, an optional topic for Paul. The gospel of the saving justice of God would lack all force and relevance were he not to demonstrate the need on the human side for the intervention of God, if he did not paint convincingly the plight of a world fallen out of relationship with its Creator. The gospel is indeed "good news." But before it can speak its positive message it has to unmask the false security and captivity which beset the human race.

So Paul spells out here a mighty "*J'accuse*," meant to lead all to conviction of sin and the conversion preceding faith. Much of what he says and his accusatory style are alien to modern sensibility. But his analysis unmasks the false securities of our world as effectively as his own. The gospel today confronts a world divided by ideologies and unequal distribution of resources, a world dehumanized by both scarcity and excess, a world living increasingly under the threat of total annihilation as its two major camps escalate weapons of nuclear devastation. The apocalyptic scenario of the "end of the world" has in this century become a possibility, not as something rained down from heaven, but arising strictly from "below," from the combination of unprecedented technological progress and continuing failure on the human side to employ that progress in non-destructive, humanizing ways. In this sense no section of Romans is more relevant or more pressing than the disturbing one which lies before us.

1:18-32: The Revelation of God's Wrath in the Gentile World

Introduction
[18]For the wrath of God is revealed from heaven upon all the wickedness of men, who in their wickedness suppress the truth.

Presupposition
[19]Because what can be known of God is plain to their eyes, since God himself has made it plain. [20]For from the creation of the world the invisible attributes of God, his eternal power and deity, have been clearly knowable through the things that he has made.

Fundamental human lapse	*God's Reaction*	*Moral Consequences*
I [21]Because, though they knew God, they did not glorify him as God or give him thanks, but they became futile in their thoughts and their unperceptive hearts were darkened. [22]Claiming to be wise, they became fools, [23]and exchanged the glory of the immortal God for the likeness of the image of merely mortal men or birds or animals or reptiles.	[24]Therefore, *God gave them up*	in the lusts of their hearts to impurity, to the dishonoring of their bodies among themselves.

II [25]Because they ex-changed the truth about God for a lie and wor-shipped and served the creature rather than the Creator, who is blessed for ever. Amen!	[26]Because of this, God *gave them up*	to disgraceful passions. Their women exchanged natural relations for un-natural [27]and the men, giving up natural rela-tions with women, burned with desire for one another, men committing shame-less acts with men and receiving in their bodies due penalty for their perversion.
III [28]And since they did not see fit to acknow-ledge God,	*God gave them up*	to a base mind and un-seemly conduct. [29]They were filled with all man-ner of baseness, evil, covetousness, malice. They are full of envy, murder, strife, deceit, ill will. They are gossips, [30]slanderers, haters of God, insolent, haughty, boasters, inventors of evil, heedless of parents, [31]foolish, faithless, heart-less and ruthless.

Conclusion
[32]Though aware of God's decree that those who do such things deserve to die, they not only do them, but approve those who practice them.

The pattern according to which the text has been set out above hinges around the curious statement, "God gave them up" occurring no less than three times (vv. 24, 26, 28). In each case it follows a statement describing a fundamental failure on the part of human beings to acknowledge God as Creator (vv. 21-23; v. 25; v. 28a) and in each case it precedes a rather lurid account of the moral consequences in human life of that "giving up" on the part of God (vv. 24b; 26b-28; 28c-31). This reiterated sequence makes up the body of the passage, with v. 18 functioning as an introduction, vv. 19-20 as a presupposition explaining why the world is without excuse, and v. 32 forming a moralizing conclusion and also a bridge to what is to come.

Wrath (1)

Paul introduces this whole section with a statement about the revelation of God's wrath (*orgê*). His language (cf. the introductory "For") suggests that the revelation of God's righteousness mentioned in the parallel statement immediately preceding (v. 17) can be inferred from this revelation of the wrath. But the precise relationship between the two "revelations" is far from clear. Where and how is God's wrath revealed and in what does it consist? To make headway with these questions we must, again, return to the Old Testament and apocalyptic background to see what concept of "wrath" Paul is presupposing.

In that tradition the "wrath of God" signifies far more than an emotional state. The prophets conceive of God's "wrath" as his intensely personal reaction to sin, emanating from him as a consuming, destructive force. In the later writings (e.g., Zeph 1:18; Pss 59:13; 69:24; Dan 8:19) there appears the conception of God's wrath as more or less detached from him: an impersonal process of sin automatically working itself out and turning into its own punishment. As we move towards the apocalyptic writings "wrath" can virtually stand as equivalent for the eschatological punishment, not so much as something inflicted by God "from above" as allowed by him to come out of the sinful situation.

There are places in Paul where "wrath" does seem to have this impersonal sense and refer simply to the eschatological punishment to come (1 Thess 1:10; 5:9; Rom 2:5, 8; 5:9; 9:22). Elsewhere (1 Thess 2:16), as here, the "wrath" seems to refer to something already present. Moreover, the reiterated statement about God's "giving them up" should caution us against taking too impersonal a view of "wrath" in Paul, at least where this passage is concerned. It is hard to escape the conclusion that Paul here portrays God as personally and decisively involved in the coming of his "wrath" upon the Gentile world and that the evidence for this, its "revelation," is to be seen in the captivity of that world to all the vices listed at such length from v. 24 onwards. Sin has become its own punishment.

The "Exchange" of Glory

Let us leave for a moment the question as to what precisely Paul understands by "God gave them up" and survey the sequence of ideas in the passage. In his introductory statement Paul says that the wrath of God is revealed from heaven upon the wickedness of men who "suppress the truth." The "truth" that is meant here is specifically the "truth" about the existence and nature of the Creator. For Paul such a refusal to "know" God is inexcusable. His accusation rests upon a standard Hellenistic Jewish theology (cf. Wis 13:3-6; Acts 17:22-31) according to which God's existence and nature as Creator can be discerned from the created world. To refuse to acknowledge the Creator in this way, not to respond by "glorifying" and "thanking" him, entails a deliberate choice. This is the core and nub, not simply of idolatry, but of all sin.

Three times Paul describes this lapse and its consequences. The first, more detailed exposition in vv. 21-23 bears closer examination. At its center is the theological idea that the role and dignity of human beings in the universe is based upon their being made in the image and likeness of God. This motif goes back to the creation account of Gen 1:26-27 and is reflected in Psalm 8 (cf. v. 5: "You have made him (man) little less than a god and crowned him with glory and honor") and receives notable development in later Jewish literature. According to this tradition, when human beings (Israel) "glorify" God, that is, acknowledge his presence and power, something of his glory (*doxa*) redounds upon them (Glory is "catching"!). On a standard principle, they become "like" to that which they worship. And this "likeness to God" or (reflected) glory forms the basis of human dignity and destiny to eternal life (cf. Wis 2:23).

Thus when Paul in v. 23 says "they exchanged the glory of the immortal God for the likeness of the image of (merely) mortal man" and various kinds of animals, he is referring to the loss of this human glory that ensued upon the refusal to "know" God. His language echoes what is said in Ps 106:20 with reference to Israel's manufacture and worship of the Golden Calf (Exodus 32). This episode, which threatened to bring down God's destructive "wrath" upon the people (cf. vv. 10-12), stands as the classic instance of all idolatry and seems to govern Paul's account: human beings "worship the creature rather than the Creator" (cf. v. 28) and, on the basis of the principle enunciated above — "you become like that which you worship" — and as a sign of God's wrath, they take on the likeness of that which they worship: merely mortal man, birds, beasts and reptiles. In place of being "God-like," they become "beast-like" and destined, like the beasts, to die. They lose, in other words, their humanity.

Paul tells this story in the past tense. He appears to be speaking of a historical and fundamental "Fall" on the part of the Gentile world. But he doubtless sees here a pattern endlessly repeated in human history. To know and honor God as God, to live out this fundamental relationship to the Creator is not an option for human beings. It is the stay and sustenance of life and dignity. All sin involves a denial of this basic truth. It means putting the creature in the place of the Creator. That is why idolatry serves as its universal paradigm.

Wrath (2)

We have been considering Paul's view of the essential relationship of human beings to God and the implications of that relationship. With this knowledge, we can return more fruitfully to the "wrath" and the enigmatic "God gave them up" phrase. Within the biblical perspective, God's wrath is activated precisely because he cannot remain indifferent to human rejection of himself. Love rebuffed ensues in anger, not indifference — an anger that demands that the reality of the relationship work itself out, even if the cost be destructive. In this context what, then, does it mean to say, "God gave them up?" Paul means that God's "wrath," his destructive reaction to human sin, consists precisely in his sitting back, as it were, and allowing the consequences of the broken relationship work themselves out in human life and character. Simply by doing nothing he lets human beings experience in their own persons and social situation the withering, the perversion and decay so graphically outlined in the catalogue of vices. To apply with J.A.T. Robinson an apt popular saying, when in his wrath God gives them up he lets them "stew in their own juice."[1]

It is in this sense, then, that the vices themselves, the disastrous moral situation outlined in the third member of the pattern, constitute the "revelation of God's wrath." They represent punishment, it is true, but not punishment rained down from heaven, as if God had to add to the miseries of mankind. The punishment comes out of the human situation and consists in the dehumanization that inevitably attends the rupture of relationship with God. What the gospel does is precisely to name this situation for what it is — the revelation of the eschatological wrath — and unmask its true cause: the suppression on the part of human beings of the truth about God.

The same gospel will also proclaim that the God who "gave them up" in his wrath is the God who now intervenes to offer rescue and salvation. In this sense the revelation of God's wrath and the revelation of his righteousness are contained within the one gospel. Both are elements of the eschatological intervention it proclaims. In the apocalyptic scenario the outburst of God's wrath is the precondition for his saving intervention and points to its imminence. That is why, presumably, Paul seems to suggest in v. 18 that the

[1] *Wrestling with Romans* p. 18.

revelation of the wrath implies also the arrival of God's righteousness. In this way the two "revelations" are related.

But for the time being the latter, positive aspect of the gospel is held in reserve. Here Paul takes the apocalyptic expectation of the eschatological wrath of God and points to its "realization" in the Gentile world. The apocalyptic writers saw the wrath as future threat, as punishment rained down from heaven. Paul sees the wrath as revealed "from heaven" (in the gospel), but actualized and verified in the human situation. Here we see a key instance of his modifying, historicizing — "earthing," we might say, — the endtime events of the apocalyptic program.

REFLECTION

Paul's inclusion of "wrath" within the one ultimately saving gospel may have some bearing upon recent theological attempts to come to terms with the "shadow" or "dark" side of God that seems to be present as an element in the total biblical revelation. Romans stands here within a genuine strand of the Old Testament tradition (cf. especially the Book of Job) that has been rediscovered and found to resonate with the religious experience of many people today. Wrath is part of fidelity — a possibility that must be there if a relationship is taken seriously. The God who is and ever will be faithful is also the God who can be experienced as destructive and demanding — or, at least, the God who is not necessarily absent from destructive aspects of life.

In particular, Paul's bringing the apocalyptic wrath down from heaven, as it were, and pointing to its realization in the present human situation may have a sombre verification in a world facing the possibility of nuclear annihilation. The eschaton has in this sense been "humanized" — placed in the hands of human beings.[2] The gospel in this context does not give assurance of other-worldly rescue and survival to an elect or faithful few. It urges men and women to consider the situation under the perspective of wrath, to return to the

[2]Cf. J. Garrison, *The Darkness of God: Theology after Hiroshima,* (London: SCM, 1982) 92-117.

relationship with God and its demands as the only hope of preserving and enhancing human life on earth.

Modern thinking will doubtless demur at the ease with which Paul, probably following Hellenistic Jewish theology, assumes that the Gentile world could and should have known God from the things that he has made. The argument here seems to rest on an unsophisticated and unjustified "natural theology." Be that as it may, Paul's basic insight that when human beings give to anything less than God the kind of dedication and self-surrender that amounts to "worship" they become enslaved by it, retains its truth. If "idolatry" in the classic religious sense is not our problem, we can write in the "idols" of our age — all that people pursue in reckless and ultimately destructive ways, whether wealth or power or drugs or success or even the inordinate desire to do good.

The whole idea of "alienation," the dehumanizing aspects of the demands of production and insatiable technological development find a foreshadowing in the words of the Psalmist:

> Their idols are silver and gold,
> the work of human hands.
> They have mouths, but they do not speak,
> they have eyes, but they do not see,
> they have ears, but they do not hear,
> noses but do not smell,
> they have hands, but do not feel,
> feet, but do not walk, . . .
> Those who make them will come to be like them,
> and likewise all who trust in them
> (Ps 115:4-8; cf. Ps 135:15-18; Is 44:9-20).[3]

Paul's perspective is broader. As we have noted, he is using idolatry as a paradigm of the essence of all sin. But he is developing the same basic biblical insight: you become "like" that which you worship — "God-like" and truly human, if you worship God; less than fully human, if you worship anything less than God. To put it another way round: God is

---

[3]Cf. J. Kavanaugh, *Following Christ in a Consumer Society: The Spirituality of Cultural Resistance* (New York: Orbis, 1981) 11-12.

the only one to whom one can give oneself with that totality of dedication that amounts to worship and retain — indeed enhance — one's humanity. All else makes for enslavement.

Paul's analysis of the plight of the Gentile world owes much, then, to this "image of God" anthropology stemming ultimately from Gen 1:26-27. Here we have the negative picture, it is true. But the dark cloud has a silver lining. Presenting the "plight" of the human race or "un-salvation" in terms of loss of humanity carries with it the positive corollary that salvation itself will consist in the restoration or rather the achievement of the fullness of humanity — not a "pie in the sky" superimposed upon human life, but its complete enrichment, in accordance with God's original and still valid design.

For Paul this salvation begins to be realized when the "not-knowing" of God at the heart of sin is reversed in the true knowing of God involved in faith. At our present stage in Romans such a positive perspective lies some way down the track. It may, however, be worth indicating a passage in an earlier letter, where the positive side is presented in a most attractive and instructive way. In 2 Cor 3:18 Paul presents the Risen Christ as the "image" or "mirror" in which, under the new dispensation, believers truly know God: "And we all, with unveiled faces, seeing as in a mirror the glory of the Lord, are being changed into his likeness from one degree of glory to another; and this comes from the Lord as Spirit" (cf. also 4:4-6). Through the knowledge of God that faith involves, likeness to God is restored/gained — and with it freedom, humanity and destiny to eternal life.

Finally, some remarks about the list of vices occurring in this passage in connection with the revelation of God's wrath. Rather than being something expressly composed by Paul, the list probably had its origin in traditional catalogues compiled in Jewish circles for apologetic purposes. This should put us on our guard against singling out individual items and attaching undue weight to their mention. Paul is not targeting specific failings here, so much as using the whole list to illustrate the perversity — personal, interpersonal and social — into which, according to Jewish thinking, the sin of idolatry has led the Gentile world.

The prominence accorded to sexual failings, especially to homosexual behavior, reflects standard Jewish abhorrence of the sexual mores prevailing in the Greco-Roman world. In such an attitude of blanket condemnation modern distinctions such as that between homosexuality as a (pre-moral) psychological disposition and homosexuality as a chosen pattern of behavior found no place. A sensitive exegesis, then, will not regard the passage simply as a quarry for biblically authenticated condemnations of specific vices. To use it as such, apart from raising wider questions about the use of the Bible in specific moral issues, would be to neglect the major thrust of Paul's argument, which is focussed, as we have seen, upon the fundamental relationship with God.

READING:

*C.K. Barrett, *From First Adam to Last* (London: Black, 1962) 17-20.

G. Bornkamm, "The Revelation of God's Wrath," in *Early Christian Experience* (New York: Harper & Row, 1969; London: SCM) 47-70.

R. Bultmann, *Theology of the New Testament* (2 vols., London: SCM, 1952, 1955) 1.288-89.

*A.P. Hanson, *The Wrath of the Lamb* (London: SPCK, 1957) 36-40, 65-67, 83-85, 110 [But cf. C.E.B. Cranfield, *Romans* 1.108-110].

G. Herold, *Zorn und Gerechtigkeit Gottes bei Paulus* (Bern/ Frankfurt: H. Lang/P. Land, 1973).

*M.D. Hooker, "Adam in Romans 1," *New Testament Studies* 6 (1959-60) 297-306.

4

The World's Need For God's Justice (II): Jews 2:1-3:20

In all that he has been saying up to this Paul would command ready assent from Jewish hearers. His portrayal of the depravity of the Gentile world adds little, if anything, to the Jewish models upon which it is based. At this point, however, he suddenly turns round to bring the Jews also under his sweeping accusation. For a time he refrains from naming them explicitly. He addresses his accusation more generally against "you who pass judgment." But from the outset it is clear that he has the Jewish world in view.

Much of what Paul is to say here about the Jewish world and the diatribe style in which his accusation is cast can sound very arbitrary and indeed anti-Semitic. But the fact that he refrains from naming the Jews explicitly at the start and speaks in more general terms of the "judger" suggests that his prime target is a specific religious attitude rather than a national group. It is the attitude of assumed religious superiority and complacency, the claim of the "insider" to privileged treatment and special consideration. Such an attitude is prone to judge harshly the conduct of those who do not belong, while apt to ignore the very real failings of one's own group or oneself.

It must be acknowledged that the early Christians saw such an attitude as characteristic of Jews who refused to accept Jesus as the Christ. This view of contemporary Judaism has left its mark on virtually all the New Testament documents and may go back, as the gospels suggest, to the conflicts between Jewish authorities, such as the Pharisees, and Jesus himself. It is, however, a religious judgment, rather than a historical one. The fact that it is recorded in the New Testament does not make it historically valid for all time. Even Paul, who by and large, stands in the mainstream of that New Testament attitude, is already moving to "typify" this attitude rather than lock it directly and permanently upon each and every Jew. What he is doing in this passage is attempting to show that, alongside a world standing in need of the gospel because it is dehumanized by its vice, there is also a world far more subtly dehumanized by its assumed superiority and complacency. For classic illustration of the latter we have only to look to the figure of the Elder Brother in Luke's parable of the Two Sons (15:11-32). It may, in fact, help to keep this example in mind.

A. God Has No Favorites
2:1-16

Introductory Accusation

[1] You therefore are without excuse, you who pass judgment, whoever you may be. For in judging another you condemn yourself, since you the judge do the very same things. [2] We know that God's judgment upon those who do such things is fair. [3] But do you suppose, you who judge those who do such things and yet do the same yourself, that you will yourself escape the judgment of God? [4] Are you presuming upon the richness of his kindness and patience and tolerance, failing to realize that this kindness is meant to lead you to repentance? [5] In your obstinacy and unrepentance of

heart you are storing up wrath for yourself on the day of wrath when God's just judgment will be revealed.

The Criterion of Judgment
⁶For God will render to each according to his works: ⁷for those who by endurance in good works pursue glory, honor and immortality, there will be eternal life; ⁸but for those who are out for selfish gain, who are unsubmissive to the truth and obey wickedness, there will be wrath and fury. ⁹Tribulation and distress await everyone who does evil — the Jew first, but also the Greek; ¹⁰while glory and honor and peace await everyone who does good — the Jew first, but also the Greek.

God Shows No Favoritism
¹¹For God shows no favoritism: ¹²those who have sinned apart from the law will also perish apart from the law; and those who have sinned under the law will be judged by means of the law. ¹³For it is not the hearers of the law who stand justified before God; rather, those who carry out the law will be justified, [¹⁴For whenever the Gentiles, who do not have the law, do by the light of nature what the law prescribes, then, though they do not actually have the law, they constitute a law for themselves. ¹⁵They show that what the law prescribes is written on their hearts, while their conscience bears witness as it stands between their thoughts that now condemn, now excuse them in continuous debate] ¹⁶on that day, when, according to my gospel, God will judge the secrets of men's hearts.

Paul begins by characterizing the Jews as those who pass judgment on the Gentile world, while at the same time, he insists (vv. 1,3), "*you do the same.*" To say that the Jews pass judgment on the Gentile world is to state nothing remarkable nor particularly offensive. To go on to say thay they "do the same," that is, share the pattern of vice just charged against the Gentile world, is to make a most extraordinary and provocative claim. It flies in the face of the mass of evidence we have from the ancient world, much of it from pagan sources, acknowledging the high moral tone of Jewish life. It is simply not true, historically speaking, to say of the Jews, "You do the same." What then does Paul mean by this curious accusation?

One way round the difficulty is to say that the sin here consists precisely in the "judging." The Jews do not actually follow pagan life-style. But their assumed position of moral superiority and judgment challenges the role that belongs to God alone. In this way they too put "the creature in the place of the Creator" and so it is true to say of them "you do the same." But this explanation will not do. Both here and throughout the entire section (cf. esp. vv. 6-13; 17-29) Paul makes it clear that he has actual failings and not merely an interior attitude in mind. The "judging" simply adds fresh culpability to sins actually committed.

What Paul is attacking here is the attitude of hypocrisy which precisely in its judging others is blind to its own failing. He swings round to trap and challenge the "judger" to look into his own life and see whether he does not do the same. Paul is not offering a historical, empirical judgment about the mores of the Jewish world as he knows it. He is rhetorically and prophetically throwing down a challenge intended to lead his hearers to conviction of sin. The whole aim is conversion — not statement of empirical fact.

To promote this conversion of heart Paul arraigns his Jewish hearers before the eschatological judgment. He sharply contests the complacent attitude which assumes that Jews, even if they sin, can as God's elect expect milder judgment. The Book of Wisdom illustrates such an attitude perfectly: "While chastening us, you chastise our enemies ten thousand times more, so that we may meditate upon your goodness when we judge, and when we are judged we may expect mercy" (12:22). For Paul there is no such indulgence on God's part with respect to sin. Jews who sin are "storing up wrath for themselves on the day of wrath" (v. 5). If God in his "kindness" has so far refrained from giving them up to the wrath revealed in the vices of the pagan world, this is not because the wrath is not for them also a threat. It is rather to give them a space for repentance and conversion. That is the special favor they enjoy. It gives no grounds for presumption.

In fact, as Paul goes on to insist, God will exercise judgment with complete impartiality. The Jews should not think they are to be in a favored position simply because they possess the law. Having or "hearing" the law is not what counts, but carrying out its prescriptions. And in this respect the Gentiles who do not have the law (of Moses) are basically in the same position as the Jews since they follow a law "written in their hearts" (v. 15).

In making performance the sole criterion of justification and in claiming that Gentiles can attain such performance apart from the law, Paul's aim is to relativize the Jewish privilege, to undermine all complacency stemming from possession of the law. Basic to the argument, however, is the principle of justification according to works — first expressed in a loose quotation from Ps 62:12 in v. 6 and then developed in positive and negative form in the following verses. How is the endorsement of such a principle at this point reconcilable with what is to be the central positive thesis of Romans that the eschatological justification is not going to be by works but by responding in faith to God's act of grace?

Is Paul simply inconsistent? Do we have a "throwback" to the mentality of his pre-conversion past? Do "works" in this context somehow "include" or even primarily mean "faith"? None of these explanations are satisfactory. We must concede that Paul does here expressly and unequivocally formulate a principle of justification according to works. At the same time we must also bear in mind that in this part of Romans he is arraigning the Jewish world on its own terms, that is, prescinding from God's act of grace in Christ. To promote conversion and compunction of heart he is bringing that world before the eschatological judgment, where, according to the apocalyptic expectation, justification is to be by works. As a Christian Paul himself knows that the gospel of the crucified means a verdict of "total failure" upon all human works. *In fact,* there is not going to be any justification granted on that basis, because "all have sinned." If there is going to be justification, it will only be because God has found a way to grant it apart from and despite this universal moral failure. That God has found a way to justification is soon to be Paul's proclamation (3:21-31). But for the present he keeps this out of sight. He is preparing the dispositions necessary for its acceptance.

But the proclamation of God's gracious work in Christ will not, when it is made, invalidate the *principle* of justification formulated here in Romans 2. As we shall see, there is a sense in which Christ (and he alone) is "justified" on the basis of his obedience, that is, on the basis of his "work." God's gracious justification consists in allowing believers to come under the scope of the justification that deservedly pertains to him. Moreover, Paul portrays subsequent Christian life as involving a continuing accountability (2 Cor 5:10; Gal 6:7-8; cf. 1 Cor 3:13-15; 9:24) and he can refer justification quite plainly to the future (Rom 5:19; 8:31-34; cf. Gal 5:5). This suggests that God's gracious justification runs its full course in Christians in so far as they "remain within" and live out in their own lives the justifying obedience of Christ. The traditional Jewish principle of accountability for one's works before God retains its validity and Paul can endorse it without embarrassment to his central proclamation. He uses it to arraign the Jews in their sinfulness and need for Christ. But it is not then laid aside. It is to play its part in his concept of Christian responsibility in the world as both response to and expression of the saving justice of God.

B. Who Is the Real Jew?
2:17-29

Basic Jewish Privilege	Presumed Role for Others
	[19]and if you are sure you are
[17] [1] If you call yourself a *Jew*	[1] a guide to the blind,
[2] and rely upon the law	[2] a light for those in darkness,
[3] and boast in God	[20] [3] an instructor of the foolish,

¹⁸ [4] and know his will   [4] a teacher of little ones
     [5] and discern good and evil,   [5] having the embodiment of
         taught *by the law*   knowledge and truth *in the law,*

The "Reality"

²¹ [1] you who teach others,   do you not fail to teach yourself?
     [2] you who preach not to steal,   do you not steal?
²² [3] you who say not to commit
         adultery,   do you not commit adultery?
     [4] you who despise idols,   do you rob temples?
²³ [5] you who boast in the law do you not dishonor God by
                                         breaking the law?

²⁴For, as it is written, *The name of God is blasphemed among the Gentiles because of you.*

Circumcision — its only value

²⁵Circumcision is indeed of value if you keep the law. But if you break the law, your circumcision becomes as uncircumcision.

²⁶If a man who is uncircumcised keeps the precepts of the law, will not his lack of circumcision be reckoned to him as circumcision?

²⁷And he who is physically uncircumcised but keeps the law, will pass judgment on you who, while having the written code and circumcision, break it.

Who is the Real Jew?

²⁸For he is not a real Jew who is one in outward appearance only, nor is real circumcision that which appears only outwardly and in the flesh.

²⁹But he is a real Jew who is one inwardly and real circumcision is a matter of the heart, governed not by written commands but by the Spirit. Of such a person the commendation comes, not from man, but from God.

Once again the text has been set out in a schematic way to show the formality of its construction. This is very evident as far as vv. 17-23 are concerned. The elements come in three groups of five. First a list of Jewish privileges or fundamental claims, then a list of what the pious Jew can hope to be for others on the basis of those claims, finally a double list stating the gap between what one teaches and what one does oneself. Note that the final or fifth element in each of the three lists makes mention of the law. Although the pattern is not carried through in the second half (vv. 24-29), the passage returns at the end to where it began, asking, "Who is a real Jew?" and responding, "The one whom God commends" (cf. v. 17: "If you *call yourself* a Jew,..."). This "chiastic" structure (that is, one where the end corresponds to the beginning) rounds the passage off as a complete unit.

The formality of structure suggests that in this passage also we do not have something expressly composed by Paul but rather a set piece of early Christian anti-Synagogue polemic. It is not, then, to be taken in all its details as representing Paul's express verdict on contemporary Jewish behavior, nor is he necessarily using it in the way it was originally intended. His intention is to challenge the Jews to see the gap between preaching and practice that affects even them. The aim is that, on the very principle of justification by works of the law which they proclaim, they will see themselves convicted and no different from the Gentiles whom they presume to instruct.

The passage forms, in fact, something of a parallel to what has just gone before. There it was possession of the law which Paul eliminated as a decisive factor in justification. Here he moves against circumcision: it counts for nothing if works do not follow; it is not necessary if the works are there without it. In both these key areas of Jewish privilege — law and circumcision — Paul is relativizing the distinctions; he is placing Jew on the same level as Gentile by making performance the sole criterion of acceptability.

In the end (vv. 28-29), as we have noted, he takes the very first claim — to be a Jew (v. 17) — and radicalizes it completely. The real "Jew" is not the one who is outwardly so, nor is physical circumcision the circumcision that really counts. The real Jew is the person who is one inwardly (lit. "in secret") and who manifests a "circumcision of heart," governed "not by letter but by the Spirit" of God. Here Paul breaks out from the "pre-Christian" perspective of this part of Romans. For just a moment he pulls aside the curtain and gives a glimpse of the rationale he will later (chaps. 6-8) provide for the possibility of a life truly conformed to God's will. The gift of the Spirit creates a "circumcision of heart," enabling a person to live a life pleasing to God in a way which commitment to the written code could never do. Such a person receives (at the eschatological justification) the all-important and solely necessary "commendation of God."

But that is for the present only a glimpse of what lies far ahead. Paul has pointed to the eschatological wrath manifest in the vices of the Gentile world, who "do not know God." He has now placed the Jews, who claim to "know God," in a virtually equivalent position, even if the wrath is for them still a threat. Though they "judge" the Gentiles, they in effect "do the same." It is performance, not privilege, that counts and on that criterion the gospel convicts all without exception. All stand in alienation from God and all suffer the dehumanization that results from lack of relationship. Only a movement from his side can break the impasse.

C. God's Abiding Fidelity in the Face of Human Infidelity 3:1-20

Objector [1]What, then is the advantage of being a Jew?
Or what value at all has circumcision?

Paul [2]Much and in every way. For, in the first place, the Jews have been entrusted with the oracles of God.

[GOD]	[HUMAN BEINGS]
	[3]What if some were unfaithful?
	Their infidelity does not nullify
the *fidelity* of God, does it?	
Obj [4]Not at all! Let God be *true,*	though every man be false,
as it is written: *That you may be*	
found righteous in all your	
words and prevail when you	
are judged.	

Paul   [5]But if our wickedness sustains
the *righteousness* of God, what
shall we say? That God is unjust in inflicting the wrath?
(I speak in a human way.)
Obj [6]Not at all! For how else could
God judge the world?

Paul   [7]But if through my falsehood
God's *truth* abounds to his glory,
why am I still being con-
demned as a sinner? [8]And
shall we then say (as some slan-
derously charge us with saying)
"Let us do evil that good may
come?" (Their condemnation is
just).

Obj [9]What then! We Jews are at a *dis*advantage?

Paul No, not at all. For we have already charged that Jews and Greeks
are all (together) under sin

(Extended Proof from Scripture of Universal Sinfulness)
[10] As it is written, *There is none righteous, not one.*
[11] *There is no one with understanding, no one who seeks God.*
[12] *All have gone aside, together they have gone astray.*
    There is no one who practices kindness, no not even one.
[13] *Their throat is an open grave, with their tongues they are treacherous,*
    asp's poison lies under their lips.
[14] *Their mouth is full of curses and bitterness.*
[15] *Their feet hasten to shed blood.*
[16] *Ruin and misery mark their tracks*
[17] *and they have no knowledge of the way of peace.*
[18] *There is no fear of God before their eyes.*

Conclusion:
[19]Now we know that whatever the law says, it says to those who fall
under its scope, so that every mouth may be closed and the whole world
brought to judgment before God. [21]Because, (as Scripture says) *From*

works of the law shall no human being find justification before him (Ps 143:2). For through the law comes (only) experience of sin.

It has been customary to see Paul in the first part of this passage (vv. 1-8) responding to a series of objections which his sharp derogation of the Jewish privileges has provoked. A fuller appreciation of the diatribe style of arguing which he employs suggests, however, that it is Paul himself who puts the questions or objections.[1] He does so in order to draw from an imaginary dialogue partner the deeper searching he requires. The aim is gradually to move the discussion from the problem of Jewish sinfulness to the whole question of the fidelity and faithfulness of God. Then this difficult passage, which has often been taken in some isolation from the rest of Romans, actually paves the way for the announcement of God's intervention in Christ, which Paul is to present in 3:21-26 as the culminating expression and vindication of the fidelity of God.

I have set out the text above in a way that attempts to illustrate the to and fro of this "dialogue." Contrary to normal practice, I have included v. 9 as a continuation of this dialogue. The layout also separates antithetical statements about God and human beings on left and right respectively. An inspection of the statements about God in the left hand column shows how the phrase "righteousness of God" (*theou dikaiosunên*) in v. 5 occurs within a series of parallel phrases that clearly indicate its meaning. The parallels occurring — "fidelity" (v. 3), "true" (v. 4), "righteous" (v. 4), "truth" (v. 7) — show that for Paul, as in the Old Testament, "fidelity" is the core element in righteousness. This indication is particularly precious, since the central affirmations about the "revelation" of God's righteousness follow on so closely (3:21-26), with the meaning, presumably, unchanged.

It is not possible to discuss in detail the intricate flow of this dialogue. The heart of the matter seems to be this. Paul

[1]Cf. S.K. Stowers, "Paul's Dialogue with a Fellow Jew in Romans 3:1-9," *Catholic Biblical Quarterly,* 46 (1984) 707-22.

begins by making the (Jewish) dialogue partner throw up his
hands and despair that any value at all remains in being a
Jew. The foregoing accusation seems to have rendered use-
less all the privileges of Israel. But with this Paul will have no
truck. God made promises to Israel (lit. "entrusted oracles"
— v. 2b); he pledged his fidelity. The Jews (Paul, v. 3, says
"some of them," perhaps thinking already of the Jewish-
Christian "remnant" who have accepted Christ) have been
unfaithful. But that does not mean the end. It does mean the
end as far as the human side is concerned — there can be no
claiming deserts or resting on privilege. But falsity on the
human side does not abrogate the fidelity of God — something unthinkable (cf. the quotation in v. 4b). In fact it serves
only to demonstrate God's fidelity all the more (v. 5). That
all is not lost, that there remains a future, despite universal
sinfulness, rests upon the abiding fidelity or "righteousness"
of God. Paul is here winding up the spring for his central
proclamation in 3:21-26 of Christ as the eschatological manifestation of the saving fidelity of God.

So it seems, then, that God has some advantage out of the
morass of human infidelity. His fidelity is thereby splendidly
displayed. But does not this imply that he is unjust then to
punish human sin (lit. "inflict the wrath," v. 5)? Why am I
still judged then a sinner? (v. 7) and does this not imply the
principle (of which Paul has falsely been accused) that we
should do evil that good (that is, God's glory) may come of
it? (v. 8). Paul vigorously drives the discussion headlong into
these objections which his thesis of universal human infidelity seems to raise. By the end of v. 8 the argument seems to
have run aground, lost amid several asides warding off false
accusations. For a proper rationale of why abundant grace
does not imply further sin we have to wait till chap. 6. Here
Paul, while admitting the objections, is content simply to
insist that a thesis of the sinfulness of Israel, in the context of
God's abiding fidelity, is theologically acceptable.

The dialogue partner gives in, but then is made to sink
into a greater pessimism about Israel than is warranted.
"Far from being privileged," he asks, "are we Jews at a

*dis*advantage?"[2] No, says Paul, for "we" (Paul) have
already charged that Jews *and* Gentiles (lit. "Greeks," cf.
1:16) are in a common bind under sin. The Jews, it is true,
share a common lostness along with the rest of mankind.
But they are no worse off. In fact they still have the privilege of holding the records of God's pledges to the human
race, the pledges which contain the hope of rescue (v. 2b;
cf. 15:7-13).

So the privileges of Israel stand. Paul will return to them
at length in chaps. 9-11. What he has been at pains to show
here we can sum up as follows:
1. The Jews stand with the Gentiles in a common
sinfulness.
2. Their chosen and privileged position does not mean that
they will escape the punitive consequences that sin entails.
God's judgment is impartial.
3. Their privilege is not, however, meaningless: in the "oracles of God" (v. 2) they bear the pledges of God's fidelity, in
which, despite total lack of faithfulness on the human side,
hope rests.

Paul clinches his accusation of universal sinfulness with
a string of scriptural quotations, culled mostly from the
Psalms (vv. 10-18). Scripture, as always for Paul, provides
God's eschatological view of the situation. The selection of
texts is, of course, quite arbitrary. But from the start Paul's
accusation has not rested on logic or empirical observation
of sin. He "works backwards" from the gospel, so to speak.
If God has made the Crucified One his Messiah, if the
world, including Israel, stood in need of such mode of
salvation, then it could only be because of universal sin. It
is the gospel, then, that points to sin, Paul's aim here is to
prepare receptive soil for its proclamation by bringing
about, in the mode of a prophet (cf. 1:1-2), conviction of
sin and conversion of heart. Such conversion can only be
worked by the action of the Spirit (cf. 1 Cor 2:1-5). The

---

[2]For this translation of v. 9 see Stowers, "Paul's Dialogue with a Fellow Jew,"
719-20.

preacher brings forward the word of God in the hope that the Spirit will move his hearers to receive it as a message that is personally valid, however unpalatable, for themselves.

Paul hopes, then, to have brought his Jewish hearers, those who are "in the law" (v. 19), to admit that, brought before the eschatological judgment seat of God, they, along with the Gentiles, would have nothing to say. The basis of this is the recognition (v. 20) that "from works of law no human being shall find justification" (Ps 143:2). On the basis of achievement, which law demands, all fail. Law brings only "experience of sin" — a throwaway line which Paul will develop later on.

It is significant that the culminating scriptural allusion in this section should be to Ps. 143. We have already mentioned this psalm when discussing the Old Testament concept of God's righteousness vis-à-vis human sin (see p. 45). We noted that what was particularly distinctive about this psalm was the fact that the psalmist, while confessing his own sinfulness and averring that "no one living is righteous before you" (v. 2; cf. Rom 3:10), calls upon God precisely in his "righteousness" to save him (at the beginning: v. 2 and again at the end: v. 11). It is highly likely that, as suggested by J.B. Hays,[3] this psalm has an important role in shaping Paul's argument in the whole of Romans 3. It presents a pious Israelite in precisely the situation to which he wishes to bring the Jews — conscious of sin, acknowledging that before God's judgement they will find no justification on the basis of works of law, yet confident nonetheless that they can invoke God's righteousness, his fidelity even to the sinner, and thereby find salvation. When straightaway in the next verse (21) Paul proclaims the manifestation of God's saving righteousness in the Christ-event it is hard to believe that he does not have the pattern of this psalm in mind.

In conclusion let us return for a moment to the *apocalyptic scenario.* We are now in a position to appreciate Paul's

---

[3]"Psalm 143 and the Logic of Romans 3," *Journal of Biblical Literature,* 99 (1980) 107-15.

essential modification. We saw that the Jewish apocalyptic expectation was that God would intervene and institute judgment. He would "justify" the faithful community on the basis of their law-righteousness, overlooking their faults in his mercy and favor. They would enter into salvation, while the sinful mass outside (the Gentiles and faithless Israelites) would be condemned. Paul is about to announce the eschatological saving intervention of God. But he insists that it is to meet a totally different situation on the human side. There is no faithful community. There is not going to be any justification on the basis of law-righteousness. All, Jews and Gentiles, are bundled together in a common bind of sin. But, precisely because God remains faithful, he is intervening in the very context of human infidelity to convert the common bind of sin into a common possibility of justification and salvation on a wholly other basis. The apocalyptic framework is there. It provides all Paul's key language and concepts. But as far as the Jewish expectation is concerned all has been turned upside down. It is this that Paul has been trying to get his Jewish hearers to see.

REFLECTION

Throughout Christian history all renewed proclamation of the gospel, every attempt to appropriate it more deeply, has been preceded by conversion, by the conviction that all is not right with oneself and one's world. The entire phenomenon of the Reformation provides striking illustration for this, culminating, in the English-speaking world, in the preaching of John Wesley. In the Catholic counterpart to that movement we find Ignatius of Loyola in his Spiritual Exercises insisting that the only after days of meditation upon personal sinfulness is the retreatant disposed to hear the more positive summons of the call of Christ. The aim is not to catalogue one's sins and rest there begging forgiveness. The goal is, rather, to gain entrance into the mystery of sin, some revelation of the subtle ways in which one's relationship to the God of freedom is out of joint. While reflection and memory play a part in this and while Scripture may prove a catalyst, such knowledge is ultimately the gift of God.

Paul's presuppositions in Romans 1-3 are similar. To some extent he "catalogues" the sinfulness of first the Gentile, then the Jewish world. But, as we have seen, these are not empirical judgments, but "accusations." They come home to the reader only in the light of the Spirit. In the categories of first the Gentile and then the Jewish world Paul suggests two shapes in which human sinfulness and alienation appear. Both lead to dehumanization. But there is the strong suggestion that the latter ("Jewish") kind is somewhat more difficult both to recognize and to heal. The recognition and the healing come in the gospel — whose central content Paul is now ready to proclaim.

READING:

*J.M. Bassler, "Divine Impartiality in Paul's Letter to the Romans," *Novum Testamentum* 26 (1984) 43-58.

*J.B. Hays, "Psalm 143 and the Logic of Romans 3," *Journal of Biblical Literature* 99 (1980) 107-15.

E. Käsemann, "The Spirit and the Letter," in *Perspectives on Paul* (Philadelphia: Fortress, 1971; London: SCM) 138-66, esp. 138-46.

*S.K. Stowers, "Paul's Dialogue with a Fellow Jew in Romans 3:1-9," *Catholic Biblical Quarterly* 46 (1984) 707-22.

U. Wilckens, *Der Brief an die Römer* (3 Vols., Cologne/ Neukirchen-Vluyn: Benziger/Neukirchener, 1978, 1980, 1982) Exkurs: "Das Gericht nach den Werken," 1.127-31, 142-46.

*S.K. Williams, "The 'Righteousness of God' in Romans," *Journal of Biblical Literature* 99 (1980) 241-90, esp. 265-71.

5

The Revelation of God's Saving Justice in Jesus Christ 3:21-31

A. God's Action in Christ
3:21-26

Re-statement of Theme

[21-22c] But now the righteousness of God stands revealed — quite independently of the law, though the law and the prophets bear witness to it — the righteousness of God, operative through the faith of Jesus Christ for the benefit of all believers.

Digression

[22d-23] For there is no distinction: for all have sinned and stand deprived of the glory of God.

Main Announcement

[24] They are being justified freely through his grace by means of the redemption which has come about in Christ Jesus.

Mode of Redemption

[25a] God put him forward so that in the shedding of his blood he might be a means of expiation operative through faith.

What this shows about God

[25b]This took place to show God's righteousness with respect
to all the sins passed over during the period of his patience,
[26]and also with a view to showing his righteousness in the
present time, so that he shows himself to be righteous precisely in his justifying a person through the faith of Jesus.

At this point in Romans Paul would hope to have convinced his hearers of the alienation from God and sinfulness
of the entire world. He would hope also to have persuaded
his Jewish brethren that the fact that Israel is part of that
sinful world and cannot hope for justification on the basis of
law does not mean an end to God's promises. Human infidelity does not abrogate the fidelity of God — to his people
and to his entire world. Paul now takes up the great positive
theme of his gospel: the announcement that God has in fact
exercised his saving fidelity. He has made his eschatological
intervention and graciously offered a renewed relationship,
with all the benefits of salvation that accrue. The theme
enunciated in 1:16-17 is restated in this "hinge" passage of
Romans. But now it includes as its core and focus Jesus
Christ, the embodiment of God's saving righteousness.

Paul makes the announcement in a lengthy, overladen
statement. There is, nonetheless, a discernible structure,
which the presentation above attempts to set out. The passage begins and closes with a double announcement of the
revelation (vv. 21-22c) or showing (vv. 25b-26) of God's
righteousness. "Sandwiched" in between is the announcement of God's gracious act of justifying believers through the
death of Christ, described in sacrificial terms (vv. 24-25a).
Preceding this is a short digression (vv. 22d-23), summing up
the lack of righteousness on the human side and consequent
need for gracious justification.

The opening statement (v. 21) indicates once more the exclusion of the law: God is not intervening in response to any righteousness on the human side stemming from practice of the law. But as *Scripture*, "the law" along with "the prophets" does bear witness to this revelation of his righteousness. At this point Paul does not cite any particular text. Later, in chap. 4, he will establish more explicitly the contention that Scripture as a whole serves the gospel, not law.

Jesus Christ and Faith

The second statement about God's righteousness contains the all-important positive qualification that it is operative through Jesus Christ and through faith. Immediately we run into some ambiguity with respect to faith. The first reference to "faith" in this verse (Greek: *dia pisteôs Iêsou Christou*) has traditionally been understood as referring to believers' faith "in" Jesus Christ. That is, Jesus is himself the object of faith. This is grammatically possible. But a more natural reading of the Greek genitive construction is to see it as referring to Jesus' own faith ("the faith of Jesus Christ"), so that he becomes the subject rather than the object of the believing. This "subjective" interpretation leaves the second reference to faith in the sentence ("all believers" — *pantas tous pisteuontas*) free to refer to believers' faith without a sense of redundancy. It also has a fine parallel in the following chapter (4:16), where the reference is certainly to Abraham's own faith, not to faith "in" him. That Paul was interested in the attitude of Christ is shown by the reference to his "obedience" in chap. 5 (v. 19; cf. "obedient unto death," Phil 2:8) and, of course, "obedience" and "faith" are closely linked ideas for Paul. These considerations, amongst others, have led a growing number of scholars to recognize that Christ's own subjective attitude before death, specifically, his own personal faith in God, may play a central role in Paul's understanding of the redemption, both here in Romans 3 and elsewhere.

An interpretation according a role to the personal faith of Jesus opens up this passage, which has always been theologically significant, in fresh and illuminating ways. To begin with, it means that there are really *three* subjects of "faith" (or "fidelity": the Greek *pistis* covers both, as we have seen) in view here. To move in "ascending" order, there is, first of all, the faith of believers (*tous pisteuontas*), then there is the faith of Jesus Christ, and finally there is the "faith" or rather the "fidelity" of God himself. God's *pistis* is, of course, something rather different from the faith of Jesus and believers in himself. It is, above all, his fidelity, expressed in the whole idea of his righteousness or saving justice (cf. the parallels between "faith" [*pistis*] and "righteousness [*dikaiosunê*] in 3:2-7; also "from faith to faith" in 1:17). Jesus Christ then becomes the focal point where divine and human faith meet. His going to death in faith and obedience is both the supreme expression of human faith in God and also the embodiment of God's saving fidelity to his world, shown in the death of his Son. Believers put their faith in the God who acts in Christ. In so doing they follow or rather are built into the faith of Christ himself.

Paul has more to say about the role of Christ in the redeeming effects of God's righteousness. Before pursuing this, however, he turns aside (vv. 22d-23) for a moment to insist once more upon the universal and equal need for a gracious justification from God. All stand in need of God's righteousness, "because all (that is, Jews as well as Gentiles) have sinned and stand deprived of the glory of God" (vv. 22d-23). This terse résumé of 1:18-3:20 is notable in that it links once again human sinning and lack of the "glory" or likeness to God, which is the foundation of human dignity and destiny to eternal life. We have seen Paul speak of this deprivation in connection with the sin of the Gentiles (1:23). Here he speaks quite generally: the loss of true humanity through alienation from God affects the entire race, Jews included.

Justification (v. 24)

Paul is now (v. 24) ready to make his main announcement as to how God is revealing his righteousness. He states the effect it is having upon all who allow it to approach them through faith: "They are being justified freely through his grace by means of the redemption which has come about in Christ Jesus." Skirting the theological turbulence that has boiled around these words over the centuries, let us keep in mind the apocalyptic frame of reference that governs Paul's language. "Justification" is that verdict of acquittal, a declaration of legal right-standing that the faithful hope to hear at the time of the eschatological judgment. It means rescue — or "redemption" — from the captivity and oppression of the present, evil time and entrance into the blessings of salvation.

Paul has excluded the possibility that such a justification could be given on the basis of human deserts — law-righteousness. He is now asserting that God, in his abiding fidelity, has found a way to grant that justification or right-standing to a sinful world. Because that world is undeserving, the justification must be granted "freely" (Gk. *dôrean* — gratis). It has to be an act of pure grace (*chariti*) on God's part — the kind of exercise of his righteousness to which the psalmist in Psalm 143 appealed. For Paul this is what God is doing in the death of Jesus.

The Role of Christ

In the first part of the following verse (25) Paul explains how it is that the work of Jesus effects or enables this act of grace on God's part, which acquits human beings of their sin and opens the prospect of salvation. His language here has played a key role in the elaboration of models of redemption in Christian theology, some heavily influenced by cultural considerations foreign to Paul's own original intention. A central concern has been to explain how the all-holy God could freely and graciously acquit human beings of their sin without exacting some cost or penalty that would show the evil of sin and so vindicate his own holiness or "righteousness" (in the sense of fidelity to himself).

Such a concern tends to fasten upon the application to Christ here of the term *hilastêrion* (translated above as "means of expiation"). In the secular Greek of Paul's day the verb form of this stem had the meaning "placate" (an angry person or a god). On this understanding it is easy to conclude that Paul saw Christ in his suffering (lit. "in the shedding of his blood") placating God's anger at human sin and so allowing his grace and mercy to operate without injury to his righteousness. This "showed" his righteousness, which could be put in question "because of his passing over of sins committed previously" (v. 25b).

This "Satisfaction" theory of the atonement, traditionally associated with the medieval theologian Anselm of Canterbury, has been widely prevalent in Christian theology. Its strength lies precisely in the sense of "satisfaction" given to the demands of order and justice disturbed. It does tend, however, to drive a wedge between the attitude of God and the work of Christ in a way that scarcely responds to Paul's theology in the rest of Romans. It is well, then, to examine more closely the language and imagery used by Paul in this statement of the redemption.

In the first place, it must be conceded that Paul is concerned about the righteousness or being of God in himself when confronted by human infidelity. He raised this issue in the "objections" occurring in vv. 1-8. His concluding statement in v. 26 shows that it continues all through to be a dominant concern. But his handling of it owes more to a biblical sense of God's way of dealing with sin than to abstract theories of the demands of justice disturbed. Of central importance here is the meaning *hilastêrion* has in the biblical tradition, whatever be its associations in secular Greek.

In the Greek version of the Old Testament (the Septuagint) *hilastêrion* (actually an adjective, though sometimes used as a noun) is used to refer to the golden cover (Hebrew: *kapporet*) placed over the Ark of the Covenant in the Temple Holy of Holies. It featured in the Day of Atonement ritual (cf. esp. Lev 16:15-16) in that the High Priest sprinkled upon it the blood of the goat slain as a sin offering on that day of forgiveness and reconciliation with God. It thus came to be seen as the focus of God's presence and of his mercy in cleansing the people from sin and reuniting them with himself (hence the traditional English translation: "mercy seat").

In connection with this ritual it is appropriate to speak of "expiation" in the sense that sin was wiped away or blotted out, but not in the sense that the deity was appeased or placated by the bloody aspect of the sacrifice. Such an idea is foreign to the Old Testament idea of sacrifice, where the initiative always remains with God. The "sin-offering," in particular, was not understood as something whereby human beings could change God, "work" his forgiveness for sin. On the contrary, it was seen as a means, given by God himself, for removing the sins which prevented his people from living out their covenant relationship with him and offering proper worship. The ritual was essentially directed, then, to the restoration of the life-giving relationship between God's people and himself. It found culminating expression each year in the Day of Atonement celebration.

It is highly likely that in using *hilastêrion* with reference to Christ Paul has the Day of Atonement ritual specifically in mind. The shedding of Christ's blood on the cross represents the last and culminating Day of Atonement, where God wipes away sin and renews relationship not only with Israel but with the entire human race. It may be recalled that the so-called "Melchisedek Scroll" from Qumran announced the "good news" (gospel) of the eschatological Day of Atonement in which God's High Priest (Michael) brings about the liberation ("redemption") of the holy community from the domination of evil powers. This provides a fine contemporary parallel to the redemptive effect of Jesus' death in the gospel proclaimed by Paul. A key difference would be that in Paul's understanding Jesus does not play the role of eschatological High Priest as in the Qumran text (the soteriology of Hebrews is closer to Qumran in this respect). Rather, the shedding of his blood in death is seen within the symbolic framework provided by the Day of Atonement ritual, in which the sprinkling of blood upon the "mercy seat" is the focus of both the mercy and expiating power of God.

If these "Day of Atonement" associations underlie Paul's reference to Christ as *hilastêrion,* then he is evidently having recourse to the Old Testament sacrificial tradition to explain how the holy and righteous God deals with the problem of sin in the community to which in his righteousness he is bound. There is, however, more to be said in this connection. In the later Jewish tradition *hilastêrion* is used in a metaphorical sense to refer to the suffering of Jewish martyrs, which is seen to have a similar expiatory effect with respect to the nation's sin. In the "martyr" theology represented in the Books of Maccabees from which our most vivid illustrations come (4 Macc 17:20-22; cf. 2 Macc 7:30-38; also Wisdom 2-4) the martyr goes willingly to his death, obedient to God's command and trusting that God will raise his destroyed body and vindicate him in the sight of his persecutors. The martyr has faith, then, that God will both "justify" and raise him. At the same time his death, as *hilastêrion,* works a wider expiation.

We have already seen that there are good grounds for holding that Paul assigns a key role in redemption to the subjective faith of Jesus. This accords very well with the application to him of *hilastêrion* in this metaphorical "martyr" sense. Jesus goes to his death obedient to the Father. His obedience consists not so much in obeying a positive command to die, as in faithfully embodying in a hostile world the perfect human relationship with God. Jesus goes to his death in faith, committing his cause to God, that is, believing that God will "justify" and raise him. His faithful obedience issuing in the shedding of his blood then becomes a *hilastêrion* or justifying means of expiation for all who are prepared to associate with it through faith.

It is possible, as many scholars hold, that Paul's presentation of Christ in these terms derives from an early Christian formula, elements of which are quoted here. The tortured nature of the syntax may indeed indicate some measure of quotation. However, to regard Paul's own theology as already distanced from such an earlier tradition to any large degree would be unwise. The idea of Christ as the faithful, obedient one may well be something in which Paul stood in steady continuity with the early tradition. His specific contribution is to present Christ as embodying, eschatologically and universally, the saving righteousness of God.

What This Shows About God

Paul's redemption statement ends with a double reference to what all this "shows" about the righteousness of God (vv. 25b-26). The first mention of this display of God's righteousness looks rather to the past and specifically to the sins of Israel — all those sins "passed over" at the time when God "in his patience" held back from inflicting the wrath upon his people. Retrospectively, so to speak, the work of Christ effects expiation for these sins, just as the Day of Atonement ritual worked expiation for all the sins of the past year. The second reference to a "showing" of God's saving righteousness has to do with "the present time," that is, the time of the eschatological "now." God's faithful action in Christ has opened up the possibility of justification and salvation for the entire world. That possibility is available wherever and so long as God's righteousness "stands revealed" (v. 21) in the gospel preaching.

Finally (v. 26b), Paul returns to the fundamental issue of what all this implies about God himself. As we saw at the beginning of the chapter, the thesis (postulated by Paul) of total Jewish sinfulness seemed to throw into question the righteousness or fidelity of God. How could his promises go through if no righteousness remained on the human side? Paul is now confident that he has shown that in the death of Christ God has dealt with sin in a way that vindicates his fidelity both to Israel and to the whole world. As in the Old Testament tradition God's righteousness always worked ultimately to liberate sinful Israel and restore the relationship, so now his gracious offer of justification in Christ represents the culminating and universal instance of his saving justice.

He is "righteous," faithful, precisely in his justifying act, creatively restoring believers to full relationship.

THEOLOGICAL REFLECTIONS

In the traditional interpretation of this passage Christ in his sufferings made payment or "satisfaction" for the legal debt incurred by the human race's sin. In the understanding outlined above, which reads Paul in the light of the biblical background, Christ is more directly aligned with the Father in the sense that he embodies the fidelity and justice of God. He embodies this, however, not as a "visitor" to the human situation from outside, but as one who treads the human path of obedience and faith and bears in his body the consequences of so doing in a sinful, unjust world. The inevitability of his death does not stem directly from the will of God. It is a consequence of obediently living out God's command to be fully and truly human in the face of a world that is alienated from God and which has allowed that alienation to be reflected in its own structures of injustice. The "necessity" for Christ to suffer stems, then, not from God, but from the condition of the world.

But precisely because Christ represents the power of God's victorious righteousness his death functions as *hilastêrion* in the biblical sense. For those who approach it in faith, it becomes the means whereby the grip of sin is broken and the essential relationship to God restored. Caught up in the dynamic of this renewed relationship, believers are likewise involved in its extension to underpin the relationships upon which the whole social order rests. The Old Testament concept of all human and social relationships as reflections and extensions of God's own *ṣedaqah* becomes a central element of the gospel in the light of Paul's understanding of Christ. For the full development of this we must wait till chaps. 6-8. But already the applicability of this more strictly biblical understanding of Paul's soteriology to the modern concern for justice should be clear.

B. Consequences: Faith the Sole and Universal Principle 3:27-31

Consequences: Faith alone [Dialogue]
27Where, then, is there room for boasting? It is excluded! On what understanding of law? One that sees it as a basis for justification through works? Not at all, but one proceeding from faith. 28For it is our contention that a person is justified through faith quite apart from works of the law.

Basis: God is One
29Or are we to say that God is God of the Jews only? Is he not God of the Gentiles as well? Yes, of the Gentiles too. 30Yes, that must follow if there is indeed only one God, who will justify the "Circumcision" through faith and the "Uncircumcision," too, by means of faith.

Conclusion
31So are we, then, doing away with the law through faith? No, God forbid! On the contrary, we are upholding the law.

Paul in this small passage returns directly to the dialogue with his Jewish partner. What are the implications in religious terms of all that has just been said concerning God's gift of justification in Christ? First of all, "boasting" is excluded. In the context in which Paul is arguing, "boasting" is the attitude of self-satisfaction in one's moral achievement, a confidence that one can stand before God and expect justification and reward on the basis of that achievement. The classic illustration would be the attitude of the Pharisee in the parable of the two men who went up to the Temple to pray (Luke 18:10-14). In view of universal sinfulness and God's offer of justification to sinners through Christ such an attitude is totally excluded.

With "boasting" excluded by what God has done in Christ, it is difficult to see what Paul is after in the second half of v. 27, when he asks (literally) "Through what law (*nomos*) is it excluded?" and replies, "Not on a law of works, but through a law of faith." Throughout chap. 3 Paul uses the word *nomos* in a rather wide range of meaning. He

seems to be able to look at the law from two different points
of view: 1. as something embodying and (as Scripture) en-
shrining the will of God for the moral life of human beings;
2. as a means of seeking to obtain acceptance (approval, "justification") from God on the basis of moral achievement.
From the first point of view he can speak quite positively of
law and find for it some measure of continuity into the new
era of grace and faith. In the second sense law is absolutely
excluded by what God has done in Christ.

It may be best to understand the second part of v. 27 as an
attempt on Paul's part to indicate something of this distinction. The law is not entirely thrown out. As a system of
self-earned justification (boasting), yes, it is. But as a way of
following God's will proceeding from faith, it is not.

The full statement of the principle of justification by faith
alone in v. 28 became the virtual catchcry of the Reformation platform and as such has drawn more attention than
almost any verse in the letter. Within Paul's argument, however, it serves to ground the principle just enunciated that
only a moral life based on faith, not on works of the law, can
be operative. Most significant is the way Paul now goes on
to deepen this tenet in vv. 29-30. If God is God of the Gentiles as well as of the Jews, if there is really only one God, as
this implies, then he cannot have "two faces," as it were,
towards the world. He must have only one principle of
acceptance or justification — that of faith. Thus from the
very heart of the Jewish faith, its strict monotheistic belief in
the "one God," Paul validates at one stroke both the principle of justification by faith alone and the universal scope of
the salvation it opens up. As C.H. Dodd aptly observes:

> He (Paul) shows here profound insight. In Judaism, as it
> developed after the Exile, the prophetic assertion of the unity
> and universality of God, and the belief that Israel was His
> chosen People lay in uneasy juxtaposition. Only along Chris-
> tian lines was the antinomy solved, and the principle of
> monotheism carried to its logical conclusion.[1]

[1] *The Epistle of Paul to the Romans* (London: Hodder & Stoughton, 1932; repr.
Fontana, 1959) p. 86.

V. 31 appears to be handling a final objection: "Are we doing away with the law, then, through faith?" In reality Paul seems to be raising a difficulty simply in order to reinforce his point. Harking back, apparently, to the distinction made in v. 27, Paul insists that in the sense of the law as the abiding expression of God's will we are in fact "establishing" it through faith. How this "establishment" occurs will become clearer in chaps. 6-8.

REFLECTION

The passage, for all its difficulties, simply spells out the consequences in human life of what has just been proclaimed about the meaning of God's action in Christ. It excludes any moral achievement that does not proceed from faith in this event. All moral effort, all attempts to "do good" can only really fulfill the creative purpose of God in so far as they proceed from the basic conviction that one is a sinner who has found acceptance and grace through Christ. All else is tainted by the "boasting" that sets one up ultimately in opposition to God. A just world is not going to be built by people confident in their technology and capacity to do good. Only when humbly incorporated through grace and faith into the saving righteousness of God is human striving creative; all else will be destructive and doomed in the end to frustration.

READING:

Rom. 3.21-26:

R.J. Daly, *Christian Sacrifice: The Judaeo-Christian Background before Origen* (Washington, DC: Catholic University of America, 1978) 134-36, 230-49.

*R.B. Hays, *The Faith of Jesus Christ* (Chico, CA: Scholar's Press, 1983) 170-74.

*E. Käsemann, "The Saving Significance of the Death of Jesus in Paul," in *Perspectives on Paul* (Philadelphia: Fortress, 1971) 32-59.

W. Kümmel, "*Paresis* and *endeixis* (both words written in Greek): A Contribution to the Understanding of the Pauline Doctrine of Justification," in *Journal for Theology and Church*, Vol. 3 (New York: Harper & Row, 1967) 1-13.

*S. Lyonnet, "The Terminology of Redemption," Part II of (S. Lyonnet and L. Sabourin) *Sin, Redemption and Sacrifice* (Rome: Biblical Institute, 1970) 61-184.

T. W. Manson, "*Hilastērion*," *Journal of Theological Studies* 46 (1945) 1-10.

*J. Reumann, "The Gospel of the Righteousness of God: Pauline Reinterpretation in Romans 3:21-31," *Interpretation* 20 (1966) 432-52.

*J.A.T. Robinson, *Wrestling with Romans* (London: SCM, 1979; Philadelphia: Fortress, 1979) 37-48.

P. Stuhlmacher, "Zur neueren Exegese von Röm 3, 24-26," in *Versöhnung, Gesetz und Gerechtigkeit,* (Göttingen: Vandenhoeck & Ruprecht, 1981) 117-35.

U. Wilckens, *Der Brief an die Römer* (3 Vols., Cologne/ Neukirchen-Vluyn: Benziger/Neukirchener, 1978, 1980, 1982) Exkurs: "Zum Verständnis der Sühne-Vorstellung," 1.233-43.

S.K. Williams, *Jesus' Death as Saving Event: The Background and Origin of a Concept* (Missoula: Scholar's Press, 1975) 5-56.

Rom 3:27-31:

N.A. Dahl, "The One God of Jews and Gentiles (Romans 3:29-30)," in *Studies in Paul* (Minneapolis: Augsburg, 1977) 178-91.

6

Abraham as Faith Person and Bearer of the Promise
4:1-25

Introduction: Background to Romans 4

Paul has now stated the core of his gospel: in abiding fidelity to the human race God is offering eschatological renewal of relationship (justification) freely and graciously in Christ to all who approach in faith. He has shown the need for this kind of justification (1:18-3:20) and stated the thesis positively (3:21-26). But, of course, it remains highly polemical. Faith-righteousness must necessarily exclude righteousness through the law. So Paul still has a battle on his hands and, in the Jewish context in which he is arguing, it is natural that the field on which it is to be played out should be that of Scripture. Since Scripture gives God's view of the situation its witness is decisive. So Paul turns to Scripture to find an example of a "faith-person" *par excellence:* Abraham.

But Abraham is far from an example chosen at random. Paul really had no option other than to claim Abraham for faith. This is because of his place and significance in the Jewish tradition. To appreciate Romans 4 we must examine this tradition about Abraham in some detail.

Abraham

Paul's handling of Abraham in Romans 4 reflects an approach to key figures of Israel's history characteristic of Jewish thought at the time. In this way of religious thinking the fate and "careers" of such figures are somehow inclusive of the nation as a whole. The patriarch's stance before God, the choices he made and the promises he received are determinative for all his descendants. Out of his "story" can be read the destiny of the nation.

We find this in the case of several figures of Israel's past — Jacob ("Israel"), for example, also Isaac, Joseph, and David. Even Adam and other "proto-patriarchs" are claimed for Israel in this way. But Abraham's position is unique. He is the "father" of Israel. His pattern of religious behavior is distinctively normative. The promises made to him by God contain the whole future of the nation, all the blessings of salvation. You cannot have Israel, especially the future, glorious Israel, without Abraham. Hence Paul, in tying salvation to faith, had to go in and claim Abraham for faith. On his examination paper Abraham was a "compulsory question."

Concerning Abraham Paul had to show two things: 1. that he was first and foremost a person of faith; 2. that it was on this basis of faith that he received the promises upon which Israel's salvation and the eschatological blessings in general rest. In this way Paul could establish that Abraham is the prototype or "father" of Christians, who as the true "Israel" of the endtime receive salvation on the same basis as he.

Paul's treatment of Abraham had to be polemic. He had not only to claim the patriarch for faith, but also to shake loose from him any suggestion of works. He had to do so in the face of the prevailing tradition, which saw Abraham as the classic exemplar of obedience and, above all, as the recipient of the circumcision command (Genesis 17), the ritual basis of the commitment to obey the law. Even Abraham's faith was understood as a meritorious work.

The key biblical evidence needed to counter this tradition Paul found in Genesis 15. There it is said (v. 6) that Abraham became "right" with God on the basis of his faith. This is stated quite apart from any mention of works and long before the introduction of circumcision, which occurs only in chap. 17. This sequence of events, giving faith priority over circumcision, is the linchpin of Paul's argument. However, to follow his train of thought in Romans 4 it is essential to keep in mind the sequence of events told about Abraham within Genesis 15.

Genesis 15

The chapter begins with a dialogue between God and Abraham (vv. 1-3). God gives an assurance in a general kind of way, but the patriarch complains that he is childless, lacking an heir, and so unable to see lasting benefit in what God is promising. Then God makes a direct promise to Abraham that he will have a son and heir and descendants as numerous as the stars of heaven (vv. 4-5). We may call this the "Son/Seed" Promise. Abraham responds (v. 6) with an act of faith in this promise, whereupon the biblical writer adds the (for Paul all-important) comment: "And it was reckoned to him as righteousness."[1] There now follows a lengthy sequence (vv. 7-20) in which God makes a covenant with Abraham according to a ritual of walking between separated pieces of slaughtered animals. The matter of this covenant is a further promise to Abraham, which may be termed the "Land" Promise. God promises to give to Abraham and to his descendants (lit. "his seed") "this" land, that is, the land of Canaan in which he is presently sojourning (cf. esp. vv. 7-8; 18-21).

Thus there are really *2* Promises made by God in Genesis 15, with Abraham's faith coming in between. We can set out the sequence as follows:

1. God promises Abraham that he will have a son (*"Son/ Seed" Promise*)

2. Abraham's *act of faith* in the promise; this puts him "right" with God

---

[1] So at least the Septuagint (Greek) translation, which Paul follows.

3. God promises the land to Abraham and his "seed" (*"Land" Promise*).[2]
This sequence is crucial to the argument in Romans 4 — though Paul complicates matters somewhat by concentrating first on stages 2 and 3 (vv. 1-12), before going back to examine the structure of Abraham's act of faith with respect of the first ("Son/Seed") Promise in vv. 17-21.

Paul's argument in Romans 4 also presupposes a certain broadening of the "Land" Promise which had taken place in the later Jewish tradition. This broadening involved two stages. In the first stage the "land" promised by God, which originally referred only to Palestine, was extended so as to include the entire (physical) earth: "inheriting the land" became equivalent to inheriting "the earth" or "the world." In a second stage and reflecting a developing eschatology, "inheriting the world" came to mean inheriting not only the present world but also "the world to come." In this way the original "Land" Promise to Abraham "and to his seed" came to be seen as containing all the blessings of salvation.[3] That is why it plays so central a role in Jewish theology. It also explains why Paul has to do battle for Abraham in Romans.

A. Abraham — A Faith Person
4:1-12

Introduction
[1]What, then, are we to say about the way our forefather according to the flesh, Abraham, appeared in God's sight? [2]For if Abraham was justified on the basis of works, he has something to boast about. But not from God's point of view.

Scripture Proof: Stage 1
[3]For what does Scripture say?
Abraham put his faith in God

---

[2]The first promise (the "Son/Seed" Promise) is a double promise in the sense that Abraham, as well as being promised a son, is promised also a large progeny. In this sense one could speak of *three* promises contained in Genesis 15 (see N. Lohfink, *Die Landverheissung als Eid* [Stuttgart: Verlag Kath. Bibelwerkes, 1967] 51-64). Paul, however, seems to hold together the two aspects of the first promise.

[3]Cf. B.J. Byrne, *'Sons of God' — 'Seed of Abraham'* (Rome: Biblical Institute, 1979) p. 157.

and it was reckoned to him as righteousness. (Gen 15:6). [4]Now to one who does work the wages are not "reckoned" as a favor (*charis*) but as something owed. [5]But in the case of the person who has no works to show but rather puts his faith in the one who justifies the ungodly, his faith must be "reckoned" to him as righteousness.

Scripture Proof: Stage 2
[6]In the same way David also pronounces a blessing upon the person to whom God "reckons" righteousness without there being any works to show for it:
[7]*Blessed are they whose crimes are forgiven and whose sins are covered up;* [8]*blessed is the man whose sin the Lord does not reckon* (Ps 32:1-2).

Scripture Proof: Stage 3
[9]Now is this "blessing" pronounced upon the circumcised only or also upon the uncircumcised? Upon the latter surely, for we are saying: *Faith was "reckoned" to Abraham as righteousness.* [10]In what state, then, was he when it was "reckoned?" In the state of circumcision or uncircumcision? He was not in a state of circumcision, but of uncircumcision. [11]And he (subsequently) received circumcision as a sign, as a kind of seal of the right-standing faith had given him when he was still uncircumcised.

Conclusion
The upshot is that he has become the "father" of all who in a state of uncircumcision have faith, in order that righteousness might be "reckoned" to them: [12]and likewise he has become the "father" of the circumcised, that is, of those of them who rely not only upon their circumcision but follow also the tracks marked out by the faith our father Abraham had when he was uncircumcised.

Paul's first task is to show from Scripture that Abraham was primarily a person of faith. After the introductory statements in vv. 1-2, he moves directly into the scriptural proof, which proceeds in three stages. In the first he goes immediately to Gen 15:6. This tells of Abraham's response of faith to God's ("Son/Seed") promise and adds the comment that this faith was "reckoned" as justifying him in God's sight. The goldmine for Paul in this verse was the link it forged between faith or believing, on the one hand, and justification, on the other. Later on (vv. 17b-22) Paul will explore more deeply the inner structure of this act of faith. For the present he is content to indicate the way in which the statement designates Abraham as a "faith-person."

The next couple of verses (4-5) tease out in a very contracted way the implications of this statement. Fastening upon the commercial term "reckoned" in the Genesis text, Paul first pictures the person who has performed some agreed amount of work according to a contract. Such a "worker" can rightly expect that a wage will be "reckoned" to him as "something owed." But what of the person who has no work to show? Such a one has no just claim to make. If anything is to be "reckoned" to him it can only be on the basis of pure favor, pure grace. What makes Paul's thought rather hard to follow here is the fact that he doesn't fully complete his illustration from human "working" before making this theological point. Thus the second case he is considering, the person who has no works to show, becomes in fact the believer or Abraham standing bereft of good works before God. All such a one can do is place his trust in a God of grace, a God who "justifies the ungodly."

With this last phrase we come upon a further key element to add to our definition of "faith" in Paul's theology. The God in whom the believer puts his or her faith is a God "who justifies the ungodly," that is a God who in his grace is willing to accept the sinner. We have previously defined faith as an attitude of discernment and surrender to the creative action of God. In chap. 3 we specified that definition so as to see faith as a discernment of God's creative act in Christ. We can now add to this: faith is belief in and surrender to the God who acts creatively and graciously in Christ to justify the sinner.

It is not at all clear how or to what extent Paul thought of Abraham as a sinner. Certainly he saw him at the stage of his career to which this text refers as having no "works" to show before God. Abraham here represents the "outsider" in religious terms, the one whose acceptance is pure grace. Above all, he represents the Gentiles, who must approach God from a similar posture. In painting Abraham in these colors Paul is taking the provocative step of making the "Gentile" stance before God somehow the norm.

In the second stage of his scriptural argument (vv. 7-8) Paul follows a rabbinical exegetical device where the witness of one text is confirmed by a second having a key word in common with the first. Here the common term is "reckoned," which brings in a quotation from Ps 32 (vv. 1-2). This psalm is significant for Paul's purpose because it recounts the experience of a person who has been led, through suffering, to recognize that he is a sinner; in this admission of sin the psalmist confesses his guilt before God and finds a wonderful experience of salvation in the knowledge of acceptance and forgiveness. This experience comes as a "blessing."

Paul sees in this "blessing" attested by the psalmist (lit. "David") the experience of the justified sinner who has found a gracious God. The psalm movingly portrays the advantages in religious terms of finding forgiveness in grace over attempts to deny one's sinfulness and claim justification as a right. The psalm also adds to the witness of the "law" (that is, the Pentateuch) given by Gen 15:6, the witness of "David," held in the tradition to be both author of the Psalms and "prophet." Thus, in the way proclaimed in Rom 3:21, both "the law and the prophets" have brought their witness to righteousness by faith.

But Paul has not yet thrown down his trump card. In the third stage of his argument (vv. 9-11) he triumphantly asks about "this blessing," this experience of justification which Abraham received. Did it follow upon or precede his reception of circumcision? The answer is clear in the sequence of Genesis 15-17. Justification came first; circumcision followed, simply as a badge or seal of the justification already found through faith.

The consequences of this are quite shattering for Jewish identity. Abraham is the "father" — with all that implies for "inheritance" — first and foremost of those who in a state of uncircumcision follow his path of faith, that is, believing

Gentiles. He is the "father" of the circumcised, the Jews, only in so far as they likewise tread the part of justifying faith. This amounts to virtually a re-definition of Israel, that is, of the end-time Israel destined to inherit the promise. To this question of "inheritance" Paul now turns.

B. Abraham — Receiver of the Promise on the Basis of Faith
4:17-25

Promise tied to Faith

[13]For the promise to Abraham "and to his seed" that he should inherit the world was not given through the law but through the righteousness that has its basis in faith.

[14]For if it is those who rely on the law who are heirs, then faith has been emptied out and the promise brought to nothing.

[15]For the law brings about wrath. Where there is no law neither is there transgression.

[16]Therefore it all had to rest upon faith in order that it might be a matter of grace and so that the promise might rest secure for *all* Abraham's descendants (lit. "seed"), not only for those who rely on the law, but also for those who share the faith of Abraham, who is the "father" of us all, [17a]as it is said in Scripture: *I have appointed you to be the father of many nations* (Gen 17:5).

Structure of Abraham's Faith

[17b]He is "father," then, in the sight of the God in whom he believed, a God who brings the dead to life and calls into being things that do not exist.

[18]In hope against hope he believed that he would become the *father of many nations,* in accordance with what he had been told: *Thus shall your descendants* (lit. *your seed) be* (Gen 15:5).

[19]And it was without any weakening in his faith that he was able to consider his own body, which was as good as dead,

seeing that he was about a hundred years old, and also the dead state of Sarah's womb.

[20]With respect to God's promise he did not waver at all in unbelief, as he gave glory to God,

[21]fully confident that what God had promised he had the power also to bring about.

[22]That is why *it was reckoned to him for righteousness* (Gen 15:6).

Christian Faith

[23]But it was not for Abraham's sake alone that the words of Scripture say *it was reckoned to him,*

[24]but for our sakes as well, to whom it was going to be reckoned, to us, that is, who put our faith in the One who raised Jesus our Lord from the dead,

[25]Jesus who was delivered up for our trespasses and raised for our justification.

Promise Tied to Faith

Paul has shown from Scripture that Abraham found acceptance and right relationship with God through faith. He now moves on to establish his second major point about the patriarch: that it was on the basis of this faith-relationship with God that he received the "promise." Let us keep in mind the sequence of events in Genesis 15. The "promise" that Paul is now referring to is the second promise, what we have called the "Land" Promise, the one that follows after the statement that Abraham has been reckoned righteous in God's sight. As the language in v. 13 ("inherit the world") shows, "promise" occurs here in the broadened sense of the late Jewish tradition, that is, as including all the eschatological blessings of salvation.

Paul's reading of Genesis 15 is that this promise was given to Abraham "and to his seed" directly following upon his justification by faith and simply upon this basis. The law played no part in the situation at all. If it had, Paul insists in the rather constricted argument of vv. 14-16, it would have had two ruinous effects. Firstly, it would have destroyed the "promise-trust" structure of human relationship to God, which alone is valid for salvation. It would have turned the relationship towards an "employment-reward" model (cf. vv. 4-5), doomed to failure because of human sinfulness and provocative ultimately of alienation from God and "wrath" (v. 15).

Secondly, a law basis for the promise would restrict salvation to the Jews, frustrating God's intent to bestow it on the entire human race. That God did in fact have the whole human race in mind when he made his promise to Abraham, Paul cleverly derives from the wording of an alternative statement of the "Son/Seed" Promise stemming from Gen 17:5 (quoted in v. 17a): "I have appointed you to be the father of many nations." Since the same word does service for "nations" and for "Gentiles" in Greek, Paul can claim here that God has expressly appointed Abraham to be the "father" of the Gentiles and that it was with them particularly in view that he has given the promise of salvation to him "and to his seed." In this way Paul claims Abraham for the whole human race. The Jews are not the sole beneficiaries of the promises but rather their privileged bearers for the benefit of all.

The Inner Structure of Abraham's Faith (vv. 17b-22)

But Paul is not yet finished with Abraham's faith. He wants to forge a link between the faith of the patriarch and those who follow his path of faith in order to come under the scope of promise. So in vv. 17-22 he explores the inner structure of Abraham's faith. This is the faith he showed with respect to the original "Son/Seed" Promise, the faith that led to his being "reckoned" righteous in God's sight. In what sort of God or in God under what predominant aspect did Abraham have to put his faith? The answer to this is controlled by his personal circumstances at the time. The promise of a son came to a man whose generative powers were "dead" in view of his advanced years and who was married to a wife, Sarah, experiencing a similar "deadness" in her womb. Granted this situation, the promise meant believing in a God, "who brings the dead to life and calls into being things that do not exist" (v. 17b), that is, belief in God specifically as *Creator*. Abraham persevered in this faith against all human hope, confident that the Creator could bring into being that which he had promised (vv. 20-21).

In describing this persevering faith of Abraham, Paul throws in a significant comment, appearing at the end of v. 20. He says that in his believing Abraham was "giving *glory* to God." We may recall that when Paul was specifying the core of "Gentile" sin in 1:19-23 he included a statement to the effect that "they did not glorify God as God or give him thanks;" they did not acknowledge God precisely as Creator. The comment here that Abraham in his believing gave "glory to God" suggests that his faith, which has to be faith precisely in God as Creator, constitutes the explicit reversal of that basic pattern of sin. Moreover, just as that refusal to glorify God resulted in the loss of the human glory or likeness to God (1:23; 3:23), so we may conclude that the "glorification" involved in Abraham's faith and in all faith modelled upon his initiates the restoration or gaining for the first time of that "glory" or likeness to God which is the basis of true humanity and the positive content of salvation (cf. the "process" described in 2 Cor 3:17-18, cited above p. 59).

Abraham: Model of Christian Faith (vv. 23-25)

Having explored the structure of Abraham's faith, Paul is now in a position to present the patriarch as paradigm or model of Christian faith. Abraham's faith in God's promise that he would have a son and heir meant believing in a Creator God, one who brings the dead to life. But Christians also believe in such a God, in that they put their faith "in the One who raised Jesus our Lord from the dead." Following then, their "father" in this pattern of faith, they are open to justification in the same way as he and also to the promise of salvation that follows upon it. Thus Paul has claimed Abraham, his faith and the promise he received, entirely for Christians. He reads out of Genesis 15 not merely a story about the patriarch "back there," but the indication of God's intent and promises for all who respond now to the Christian gospel with faith.

In his final statement in the chapter (v. 25) Paul gives a concise summary of the gospel, probably derived again from an early formula of faith:

"(Jesus our Lord),
   who was delivered up for our trespasses
      and raised for our justification."

That the death of Jesus should be related to the removal of "our trespasses" comes as no surprise after 3:24-26. It is perhaps more striking that "our justification" should be associated with God's "raising" of Jesus. The implications of this are, in fact, quite significant. Discussing Rom 3:21-26 we noted that Paul's language about faith ("faith of Jesus") suggested that he was interested in the subjective attitude of Jesus in the face of death and indeed assigned a role in the redemptive process to Jesus' own faith. If Jesus, the obedient one, went in faith to his death placing his cause solely in God's hands, then his resurrection represents God's public, bodily vindication of his righteousness, his "justification" in the classic Jewish sense. Therefore Christ was raised in the first order "for his own justification." How was he raised "for our justification"? He was raised for our justification in the sense that God graciously allows believers to associate with Christ and come under the scope of the justification which he, as the obedient one, received. They do not, as Christ does, merit justification. But because his death works a wider expiation (*hilastêrion,* 3:25) they are caught up in God's act of justifying him, even if his risen life is yet to run full course in them.

It is noteworthy that Paul does not present Abraham's faith as the paradigm or precursor of the faith of Christ. That could not be, because Abraham as in some sense "ungodly" has to put his faith in a God who graciously justifies the sinner and Christ "knew no sin" (2 Cor 5:21).

Abraham models the appropriate response to what God is doing in Christ. He shows that one must approach the gospel from the stance and conviction that one is a sinner who has to rest entirely upon God's grace. This builds a grace relationship with God that alone sets one in the line of salvation and brings the believer into the worldwide scope of God's saving purpose.

REFLECTION

Following Genesis, Paul presents Abraham as a man who longed for a future — a future for his family, but also for the world. He heard God's promise of a future but saw also an immense blockage — his sterility — which only the creative power of God could overcome. Because Abraham really let God be God in his life, because he offered God faith and trust (Genesis 15) *before* setting about his "works" (Genesis 17), his entire career was able to be built into the worldwide scope of the Creator's saving power. In Christ God activates the promise concerning the world's future originally made to Abraham. In Abraham he shows how the world must respond to that promise if it is to be effective. It is God alone who as Creator can give salvation or build the future of the world. There is indeed scope for human cooperation but to be effective it must proceed from the faith and persevering hope shown by Abraham.

READING:

*C.K. Barrett, *From First Adam to Last* (London: Black, 1962; New York: Scribners) 22-45.

K. Berger, "Abraham in den paulinischen Hauptbriefen," *Münchener Theologischer Zeitung* 17 (1966) 47-89.

*B.J. Byrne, *'Sons of God'— 'Seed of Abraham'* (Rome: Biblical Institute, 1979) 68-70, 157-61.

N.A. Dahl, "Promise and Fulfillment," in *Studies in Paul* (Minneapolis: Augsburg, 1977) 121-36.

R.B. Hays, "'Have we found Abraham to be our forefather

according to the flesh?": A Reconsideration of Rom 4:1,"
Novum Testamentum 27 (1985) 76-98.

*E. Käsemann, "The Faith of Abraham in Romans 4," in
Perspectives on Paul (Philadelphia: Fortress, 1971; London:
SCM) 78-101.

W. Neil, "God's Promises are Sure," *Expository Times* 69
(1957-58) 146-49.

7

The New Basis for Hope
5:1-21

There is a distinct change of atmosphere as we pass from chap. 4 to chap. 5 of Romans. The polemical tone gives way to one of hope and exhortation. Confident that the struggle for justification by faith lies behind him, Paul now turns to the promise the gospel holds out for the future. This perspective, already anticipated in the promise to Abraham discussed in chap. 4, remains dominant right up to the end of chap. 8. God in his saving fidelity has found a way of dealing with the infidelity and sinfulness of the human race. What now is the hope that the full working out of his fidelity has in store for believers and the world?

In following Paul's argument from here on it helps to keep in mind the Christian modification of the apocalyptic perspective which he presupposes. Where the Jewish eschatology envisaged a strict separation between the present age and the age to come, the Christian perspective was, as we have seen, more complex. Since Christ represents the eschatological intervention of God, the new age has already begun. As far as relations with God are concerned, believers already, through justification, enjoy its fruits. But their possession is not complete. *Bodily* they are still anchored in the old era and suffer still its buffets and trials. Full bodily entrance into the new age will only come with resurrection. In the meantime Christians have to live in a situation where the two ages, the old and the new, overlap. Each stakes its claim and each exercises its pull.

In this situation Christian life means holding to and living out the relationship with God appropriate for the new age in the physical conditions of the old. It means walking a kind of tightrope between two opposing temptations — not succumbing, on the one hand, to the allure and the despair of the old age as though nothing had happened; not imagining, on the other, that one is wholly entered into the new age, lifted up and away from the suffering, toiling world, one's personal salvation complete. Paul's whole endeavor in this section of Romans (chaps. 5-8) could be summed up as an attempt to preserve the balance, to foster the art of living in this "overlap" situation where Christians find themselves and their world here and now.

This is why the section begins (5:1-11) and ends (8:14-39) with "hope" as the predominant theme — and hope specifically addressed to a situation of suffering. If the old eschatology clings too strongly, the experience of suffering will bring on the temptation to believe that the conditions of the old age still prevail, that one remains under the frown of God. Does not suffering indicate God's disfavor? How can sufferings have a place if the new age has already dawned? Do we not still have to earn a justification in the eyes of God? To counter these temptations, so ruinous for all that he has established, Paul has to confront the reality of suffering in Christian life and find some place for it in the post-justification era.

A. Hope in the Context of Suffering
5:1-11

Introduction

[1]Justified, then, by faith we have peace with God through our Lord Jesus Christ. [2]It is through him that we have access

also to the situation of grace in which we stand, where we can boast in the hope of obtaining the glory of God.

Suffering

[3]Not only this, but we can boast even in our sufferings, knowing that suffering produces endurance, [4]and endurance produces a tested character and such a character produces hope.

Theme

[5]And such a hope is not going to let us down, because God's love has been poured out into our hearts through the Holy Spirit which has been given to us.

The "Logic"

[6]For it was while we were still helpless that Christ died at the appointed time for sinners. [7]Now it is only with difficulty that one could die for a deserving person — though perhaps for a really good person one might be prepared to die. [8]What proves God's love for us is that it was while we were still sinners that Christ died for us. [9]How much more, then, now that we have been justified through the shedding of his blood, shall we be saved from the wrath! [10]For if when we were his enemies we have been reconciled to God through the death of his Son, all the more, now that we are reconciled, shall we be saved by his life.

Conclusion

[11]Not only do we have this hope, but we can boast in God through our Lord, Jesus Christ, through whom we have now received this reconciliation.

Paul begins by setting justification firmly behind the Christian. The dominant image is that of reconciliation and peace. Like ambassadors ushered into the presence of a ruler of a previously hostile, now firmly allied power, Christians stand confidently in an atmosphere of grace and favor. That describes the present. But, more importantly, the present grace is replete with hope. It is significant that in first mentioning this hope (at the end of v. 2) Paul characterizes it as "hope of obtaining the glory of God." We have noted how this theme of "glory" makes a small but significant appearance in all the major sections of the letter treated so far (1:23; 2:6,10; 3:23; 4:20). The "hope" that Paul envisages here is not simply hope for salvation in a vague and generalized sense. It is the specific hope for human beings of attaining in full measure that likeness to God or true humanity intended by God from the start, lost through sin but realizable now in Christ.

Introducing the theme of suffering, Paul adopts a challenging, almost defiant tone and postulates that Christians "boast" even in their sufferings. The chain-like sequence in rather Stoic vein which he uses (in vv. 3-4) to ground this thesis will not convince many who find that suffering induces despair rather than hope. Though well qualified from personal experience to speak on suffering, Paul can hardly mean that hope emerges from suffering in a kind of automatic process. But in the context of a firm belief that one stands in a milieu of grace, caught up in the unfolding of God's eschatological plan, then perhaps suffering can be seen as part of a process leading to final freedom and salvation. Such a vision stems from faith and is ultimately the gift of God. Paul will treat of suffering more amply in chap. 8.

The Spirit

In the meantime he indicates (v. 5) what is for him the key factor in producing Christian hope: God's gift to believers of the eschatological Spirit. In the Old Testament and Jewish tradition "spirit" denotes the felt presence of the creative power of God. The apocalyptic tradition saw the Spirit as the eschatological gift *par excellence*. The Spirit was to be the creative force of the new creation, as it had been of the old (Gen 1:2; 2:7). Through the Spirit the eschatological community was purified of sin, cleansed and readied for the life of the new age. The abiding image was that of water —hence the "pouring out" language in v. 5 (cf. 1 Cor 12:13: "We have all been made to drink of the one Spirit"). But "Spirit" above all constituted a deeply personal experience of the relationship to God characteristic of the new age (cf.

Ezek 36:27-28: "And I will put my Spirit within you,... You shall dwell in the land which I gave to your fathers; and you shall be my people and I will be your God"; cf. 37:12-14). The Spirit attests the reality of justification and the assurance that one stands in God's grace and favor.

The "love of God" that has been "poured out into our hearts" through the gift of the Spirit is not, then, our love for God (though in due course that will flow in response) but the felt experience of God's love and favor towards us. The gift of the Spirit represents a "coming-home" to the final relationship to God. It is a pledge of the coming-home to full (bodily) salvation which will eventually flow from that relationship. When the Spirit is around the new age is dawning. In this sense the Spirit is for Paul the key factor engendering hope in Christian life.

The statement in v. 5 about the hope flowing from the gift of the Spirit functions as a kind of theme for chap. 5, resumed and developed in chap. 8. It leads directly into a series of statements in vv. 6-10 where Paul sets up the logic which is to underpin his thought throughout chap. 5. On a kind of *a fortiori* argument, reflecting a standard rabbinic technique, the statements reiterate the same basic proposition proceeding from the extremity of God's love: if when we were sinners, that is, his "enemies," God gave up his Son to die for us and reconcile us to himself, how much more (Greek: *pollôi mallon*) now that we are his *friends* (through justification) will he not complete the process and lead us to full salvation? The force of the argument lies in the consideration that what God has done in the harder case (bringing us from sin to justification), he will surely complete in the easier (moving us on to full salvation). Thus Christian hope rests upon the love and fidelity of God.

A Parable

A young man of slender means is engaged to be married to the daughter of a wealthy business man. At the start of the engagement the father disapproves of him entirely and only grudgingly consents to the marriage. Love for his daughter induces him, nonetheless, to give the couple a very handsome engagement present — an expensive car. As the engagement goes on, however, father and prospective son-in-law become better acquainted, find they have interests in common and eventually a real friendship grows. As the marriage day approaches, we might well imagine the young man, in a way which bears some affinity to Paul's "logic" in Romans 5, reasoning to himself along the following lines: if her father, when we were simply engaged and he could not stand the sight of me, nonetheless gave us so lavish an engagement present, what may we not expect as a wedding gift now that I have his approval and am indeed a good friend? May we not think of a beach house or something similar?

So much for the essential pattern of Paul's argument. Now a few details in passing. In v. 9 Paul speaks of our being saved "from the wrath." Most translations attempt to clarify the sense of "wrath" by adding "of God." But this is not justified by the Greek, which speaks simply of "wrath," probably in the sense of the eschatological fate threatening unbelievers. In the context where Paul is emphasizing the grace and love of God, the distancing of wrath from God is likely to be deliberate. Secondly, the passage is remarkable for the absolute continuity between the action and love of Christ and the intention and love of God (cf. esp. v. 8). As in 3:24-26, the initiative for Christ's loving act flows entirely from God and embodies his love. Finally, we may note a further indication that the resurrection of Christ plays a direct role in salvation: we are "reconciled" by Christ's death; we shall be (fully) saved "through his *life*" (v. 10; cf. 4:25).

B. Christic and Adam: The Solidarity in Life Outweighs the Solidarity in Death 5:12-21

B. *Christ and Adam: The Solidarity in Life Outweighs the Solidarity in Death 5:12-21*

["ADAM" SIDE]

["CHRIST" SIDE]

¹²Therefore, as sin entered the world through one man and through sin death, and so death passed to all, because all sinned -

[¹³For sin was indeed in the world before the law was given, but sin is not booked up in the absence of law. ¹⁴Yet death reigned from Adam until Moses, even over those whose sinning did not follow the pattern of the transgression of Adam, who was a type of the one to come.]

¹⁵But the free gift is not like the transgression:

For if through one man's tres-pass many died,

much more have the grace of God and the gift in grace of the one man Jesus Christ abounded for many.

¹⁶And the free gift is not like the effect of that one man's sin:

For the judgment following that one transgression brought condemnation,

but the free gift following many trespasses brings justification.

¹⁷For if, through one man's trespass, death reigned through that one man,

much more will those who accept the overflow of grace and the gift of righteousness reign in life through the one man, Jesus Christ.

¹⁸Therefore, as one man's trespass led to condemnation for all,

so also one man's act of justice leads to freedom and life for all.

¹⁹As through the disobedience of one man, many were made sinners,

so through one man's obedience many will be found righteous.

²⁰The law came in only to multiply the trespass. But where sin increased, grace abounded all the more,

²¹so that, as sin reigned in death,

grace also might reign through righteousness for eternal life through Jesus Christ, our Lord.

Paul has insisted upon the grounds for hope in the face of suffering. Now he prepares to confront a factor in the human condition more formidable still: the reality of death. He does so with the aid of an extended comparison between Christ and Adam, which is at once the source of both the theological richness of this passage and the difficulties it raises for interpretation.

The Christian theological tradition, fastening upon the "Adam" side of Paul's equation, has read out of this passage primarily an account of the onset of sin and death, specifically a theology of "original sin." The manner in which Paul sets out his comparison is conducive to such a view. But "Adam" and the onset of sin are not the primary focus. This lies on Christ and the effects of his righteous act for the benefit of the human race. To be more precise, Paul continues to affirm here the hope that wells up for the Christian from the consideration of God's love, but he does so with greater attention to the role of Christ as the instrument of that hope. He wants to assert that the forces for life released by Christ far outweigh all that pulls in the opposite direction, seen here as released by Adam.

The "Adam" Tradition

Most of what Paul says here about Adam was already to be found in certain strands of the Jewish tradition. Where an earlier view had tended to whitewash the father of the human race and claim him for Israel as proto-patriarch, we find in the later literature (4 Ezra; 2 Baruch) a negative picture of Adam, more in line with the original tradition of Genesis 3. Here Adam's sin unleashes a legacy of sin and death upon all his descendants.

However, while attributing this legacy to Adam, the tradition never so stressed it as to eliminate from human sinning all sense of individual responsibility. It preserved and acknowledged a tension between the fate held to stem from the patriarch and the effects of individual personal sin. The author of 2 Baruch puts it well: "For though Adam first sinned and brought untimely death upon all,... each of us has been the Adam of his own soul" (54:15-19).

Despite this inbuilt tension, the "Adam" tradition provided Paul with something of great significance for his purpose: the idea of one individual having universal significance for the race in that his fate or career is determinative for all. In the case of Adam, of course, the universal significance is for ill — a legacy of sin and death. But this negative role of Adam can serve Paul as a foil for what he wants to affirm positively about Christ. In one key respect, and in that alone, Adam and Christ are like figures: each has a universal significance for the human race. In every other respect they are unlike —most notably in the effects they bring: in the one case sin and death, in the other righteousness and (eternal) life.

The Two Legacies: Adam and Christ

So Paul constructs here a sustained comparison between the work of Adam and that of Christ. The text has been set out above in a way intended to show the balanced series of statements containing the negative and then the positive side. But, as the setting out also shows, Paul has not made things easy in that in the very first statement of the comparison (in v. 12), he breaks off after stating the negative side, postponing the corresponding positive statement about Christ. For the full, balanced presentation including both the "Adam" and the "Christ" sides we really have to wait till v. 18.

Paul breaks into the comparison, in the first place (vv. 13-14), to indicate that the period between Adam and Moses, when the law had not yet been given, shows that death must have come as a legacy from Adam. This must have been the case since it is only through the law that individual sinning is "booked up" for punishment and so attracts the penalty of death. If death prevailed also in this period, as it did, this can only have been so on the basis of a legacy stemming from Adam. The reasoning here is obscure and, outside Paul's idiosyncratic view of law, unconvincing. But it serves to establish his fundamental objective, which is to use Adam to say something about Christ. As the one who through his (sinful) act brings to all a legacy of death, Adam serves as a "type" (end of v. 14) or rather "antitype" to Christ, who brings for all the possibility of life.

It seems, however, that Paul becomes nervous lest the comparison he is mounting between Adam and Christ be taken too far. In one respect — that of universal significance — Adam is the "type" of Christ. In every other respect he is "antitype." In vv. 15-17, before resuming the full statement, Paul moves to point out the difference. Where Adam represents simply a sinning human being, albeit one of universal significance, Christ embodies the "overflow" of the grace of God (v. 15). Where Adam's act took place on neutral terrain, so to speak, and unleashed a pattern of condemnation, Christ's involved the invasion of God's grace into the massive accumulation of human sin and its conversion to right-standing and grace. The "weighting," therefore, the "much more" (*pollôi mallon:* vv. 15, 17; cf. 5:9, 10), lies decidedly upon the side of grace. And the upshot is that the reign of death inaugurated by "one man" is supplanted by the "reigning in life" of those who "accept the overflow of grace and the gift of righteousness of the one man, Jesus Christ" (v. 17).

We note here again the absolute continuity expressed in these statements between the act or "gift of love" of Christ and the grace of God. This is so much the case that the actual contrast being made is not so much one between Adam and Christ as one between Adam and the grace of *God,* operative in Christ. That is, the key contrast is between a human being "going it alone" apart from God (and entraining thereby a legacy of death) and a human being totally the vehicle of God's grace (and entraining thereby a legacy of life).

Paul does eventually (v. 19) fasten upon the subjective attitude of Christ, contrasting his "obedience" with the "disobedience" of Adam. But, as we have noted in connection with Rom 3:25, the obedience of Christ does not necessarily consist in his obeying a positive command handed down from God. Phil 2:8 describes Christ as "obedient *unto* death," rather than "to" anyone or any command. This suggests that here, too, Paul regards Christ's obedience as consisting in his faithful embodying in the human condition, unto death and at the cost of death, the fidelity or justice of God. The effect is that the reign of sin is supplanted by the reign of grace through righteousness for eternal life (v. 21).

The "Adam" Story: Sin and Death

Paul's language in this final verse (21) gives us some clue as to the way he is picturing the realities of sin and death, on the one hand, and righteousness, life and grace, on the other. He is personifying them and seeing them as "powers" which exercise lordship over the human condition for good or ill respectively. Such personification undoubtedly lends a somewhat mythological tone to the entire discussion. But in the case of "*Sin*," for instance, it enables Paul to reach into the depths of human character in an attempt to grasp the root cause or core of sin. "Sin" (*hamartia*) does not refer primarily to individual sinful acts ("sins"). It denotes, rather, a subtle, willed selfishness, the fundamental tendency in human beings to place self and the perceived needs of self in the position that should only be occupied by the life-giving sovereignty of God.

Paul sees Adam's "snatch" at life (Gen 3:1-7) as giving entrance to "Sin" into the human domain and also as typifying all subsequent human lapses under its control (cf. God's words to Cain: "If you do well, you are accepted; but if not sin is [an animal] crouching at the door; it shall be eager for you, but you must master it" [Gen 4:7]). In line with the understanding of his day, Paul undoubtedly thought of Adam as an individual historical figure, the first father of the race. But Adam was more important as a type or model of sinful humanity. "In" Adam it is possible to portray the continuing "sin story" of human existence, the story of human beings going it alone apart from God, snatching life as something to exploit for selfish ends, causing and incurring thereby the death-dealing consequences which flow from that exploitation.

In presenting Adam as the paradigm or model of human sinning, Paul shows clearly that the "sin" he has in mind in this passage is the conscious personal sin of human beings. The theological tradition stemming from Augustine which found here "original sin," in the sense that all human beings somehow sinned (pre-consciously) "in" Adam, is based upon a translation of the concluding relative clause in v. 21 that cannot be sustained. Yet in seeing the source or "origin" of sin as somehow supra-individual and engrained in the race, that tradition was indeed faithful to Paul and in this respect should not be overthrown. Paul's concept of Sin as a power "let loose" in the human situation implies in some sense a solidarity in human sinning which both precedes each individual's moral history and has it effect upon it. No one sins entirely alone and no one sins without adding to the collective burden of mankind. Certainly, neither history nor the present shape of world events give any grounds for rejecting the theological view that human beings are locked in a common bind of evil, which unaided they appear helpless to cast off.

So much for sin. But what of sin's grim associate in this passage: *death*? As we have noted, Paul employs a certain strain of the Jewish tradition which did not accept death simply as the natural term of human existence but regarded it as the consequence, indeed the punishment of human sin. This is not a biological but an existential and ultimately theological evaluation of death. Yet to say, as many do, that Paul has in mind here not so much physical death as death in the spiritual sense of ultimate separation from God robs the passage of much of its force. Paul is not maintaining here that physical death follows sin as punishment according to some divine decree. The concept of "punishment" is hardly to the fore at all (if anything it is associated with the law, which Paul discounts). Rather, Paul's intent is to point out how death *follows* sin. He uses the "Adam" story to indicate that human sinning unleashes forces of death, which only the God of life can stem.

The "Christ" Story:
Grace, Righteousness and Life

But, as we noted at the start, the primary focus of this passage lies not upon Adam, sin and death but upon the force for life unleashed by God in Christ. The fatal sequence: Adam — Sin — Death (for all) is countered by the sequence: Christ (God's grace) — Righteousness — Life. Christ represents the triumphant invasion of grace into the human bind of captivity to sin. Through association with him believers receive the power to break with sin and submit instead to the life-giving sway of the grace and righteousness of God.

Thus alongside the "Adam" or "sin" story that has been told and continues to be told about human life, there has come to be a ("much more") powerful "grace" story leading to life. The "story" is told "about" Christ, that is, it is told in terms of his historical life and resurrection, but it is told truly about all subsequent believers because of what God has given to the world in him. If they allow the costly obedience of Christ to be reproduced in their lives, then they too can serve as vehicles for the disarmament of sin and death and the enhancement in the world of the life-giving reign of grace.

We said at the start that the "Adam" or negative side of this passage has drawn more attention than the emphasis it places upon Christ and life. It is important to correct this impression and to note that, not merely do we have a juxtaposition of the forces, so to speak, but a firm "weighting," a "much more," attaching to the positive side. Without this weighting the passage would simply indicate a struggle, a conflict, an equilibrium of force affecting human moral life. But Paul's central aim is to point to hope — a hope that springs precisely from the fact that the struggle *is* uneven, that the grace of God, the saving righteousness of God, does triumph over human sin, even if that triumph is not yet complete. In Christ God has given a new "patriarch" to human beings. He has refounded the human race. He has both demonstrated and enabled the possibility of being truly human, which for Paul involves the conquest of death and all that makes for death in our world.

REFLECTION

The passage we have been considering presents a powerful vision of the world as a field upon which forces for life and forces for death are locked in conflict. Though rooted in the act of Adam and that of Christ respectively, the conflict is not simply one that took place "back there," but one that continues till the end of time. Paul points to two "stories" being told about the human race. The freedom of human beings allows a "sin/death" story to be told and so the making of a humanity hastening to destruction. The grace of God, renewing creation in Christ, allows a (more powerful) "life" story to be told, one that makes for true humanity and the hope of life with God.

The choice before men and women, both individually and collectively, is "Which story are you going to let be told in your life, in your world? Are you choosing death with Adam or life with Christ?" Not only selfish exploitation but even the attitude of "going it alone" apart from God, no matter how well intentioned, ranges one inevitably upon the side of Adam. Surrender to God's gift of righteousness through faith leads to life and to becoming with Christ an instrument of life. This latter possibility Paul now takes up.

READING:

Rom 5:1-11:

*N.A. Dahl, "Two Notes on Romans 5," *Studia Theologica* 5 (1951) 37-48; included in revised form in "The Missionary Theology of the Epistle to the Romans," in *Studies in Paul* (Minneapolis: Augsburg, 1977) 70-94, esp. 82-83, 88-90.

J.A. Fitzmyer, "Reconciliation in Pauline Theology," in *To Advance the Gospel* (New York: Crossroad, 1981) 162-85.

E. Käsemann, "Some Thoughts on the Theme 'The Doctrine of Reconciliation (*Versöhnungslehre*) in the New Testament,'" in *The Future of Our Religious Past: Essays in Honour of Rudolf Bultmann* (New York: Harper & Row, 1977) 49-64.

*R.P. Martin, *Reconciliation: A Study of Paul's Theology* (Atlanta: John Knox, 1980) 135-54.

Rom 5:12-21:

M. Black, "The Pauline Doctrine of the Second Adam," *Scottish Journal of Theology* 7 (1954) 170-79.

J. Cambier, "Péchés des hommes et péché d'Adam en Rom V. 12," *New Testament Studies* 11 (1965-66) 217-55.

C.E.B. Cranfield, "On Some of the Problems in the Interpretation of Rom V. 12," *Scottish Journal of Theology* 22 (1969) 324-41.

F.W. Danker, "Romans v. 12. Sin under Law," *New Testament Studies* 14 (1967-68) 424-39.

*W.D. Davies, *Paul and Rabbinic Judaism* (4th ed., Philadelphia: Fortress, 1980) 31-57.

J.D.G. Dunn, *Christology in the Making* (Philadelphia: Westminster, 1980; London: SCM) Chap. IV: "The Last Adam," (pp. 98-128).

*M.D. Hooker, *Pauline Pieces* (London: Epworth, 1979; = *A Preface to Paul,* New York: Oxford University, 1980) 36-52.

E. Jüngel, "Das Gesetz zwischen Adam und Christus," *Zeitschrift für Theologie und Kirche* 47 (1950) 313-60.

S. Lyonnet, "Le Péché originel en Rom 5, 12," *Biblica* 41 (1960) 325-55.

*R. Scroggs, *The Last Adam* (Philadelphia: Fortress, 1966; Oxford: Blackwell) 76-82.

D. Stanley, "Christ, the Last Adam," in (M.J. Taylor, ed.) *A Companion to Paul* (New York: Alba House, 1975) 13-22.

A.J.M. Wedderburn, "The Theological Structure of Romans V. 12," *New Testament Studies* 19 (1972-73) 339-54.

8

Living-Out the Justice of God
6:1-7:6

A. Dead to Sin, Living to God in Christ
6:1-14

Introductory Objection
[1]What, then, are we to say? Are we to remain in sin so that grace may have even greater scope?

Rejection & Thesis
[2]God forbid! How can we who have died to sin continue to live in it?

Grounding: Baptismal Union with Christ
[3]Or do you not know that inasmuch as we have been baptized into Christ we have been baptized into his death? [4]We have been buried therefore with him through baptism into his death, so that as Christ has been raised from the dead through the glory of the Father, so we, too, might walk in newness of life.

Sequence 1
[5]For if we have been conformed to the likeness of his death, so we shall be conformed also to the pattern of his resurrection. [6]We know that our former human existence has been

crucified along with him to take away the body of sin, so that we are no longer slaves to sin. [7]For a person who has died is legally free from sin.

Sequence 2
[8]But if we have died with Christ, we believe that we shall also live with him. [9]We know that Christ, once raised from the dead no longer dies; death has no power over him any more. [10]For in his death he died once and for all to sin, in his (risen) life he lives to God.

Conclusion
[11]So you too should consider yourselves to be dead to sin, but alive to God in Christ Jesus. [12]Do not, then, allow sin to reign in your mortal body to make you obey its desires [13]and do not offer your members to sin as instruments of wrong-doing. But, instead, offer yourselves to God as people brought back to life from the dead and your members to God as instruments of righteousness. [14]For sin will rule you no longer, because you are not under law but under grace.

Paul now embarks upon a long excursus devoted to Christian behavior (6:1 – 8:13). It is not so much an exhortation to right living as a fundamental attempt to establish that a new moral life is both demanded and rendered possible in the milieu of grace. Why does his argument now take this tack? In the preceding passage Paul has insisted very strongly upon the prevailing power of God's grace in the face of human sin. Now if God has met past human infidelity with such generosity, there may be a temptation to think that continued wrongdoing might find similar indulgence. This somewhat naive conclusion, expressed in the objection at 6:1, may appear at first sight to come from a libertarian gleefully anticipating a moral free-for-all. But more likely Paul is moving to counter a moral zealot, who, seeing that such a conclusion might be drawn, raises it as a difficulty against Paul's overall case. With the moral straitjacket of the law removed and such emphasis upon grace, what is there left to restrain wrongdoing?

Paul's response will involve a good deal of discussion about the law. He will insist, in fact, that its removal, far from being a problem, actually constitutes the solution! In the meantime and more positively, he has to find a basis for Christian ethics in this curious "in-between" period posited by his eschatology, where the judgment is fundamentally over but where entrance into full salvation remains a hope. He has to walk a tightrope between re-erecting a law-based system of morality, on the one hand, and allowing Christians to believe, on the other, that "anything goes" since all moral accountability before God belongs to the past. His solution is to erect a system of ethics based entirely upon the union of Christians with Christ, — or, more precisely, one based upon the fact the new union with Christ involves a break with the old servitude to sin ("in Adam") so complete that it can only be described in terms of "death" to the old existence. This is summed up in the thematic question of v. 2: "How can we who have died to sin continue to live in it?"

The passage that follows (vv. 3-14) appears somewhat repetitive and loosely organized at first. But a structure can be discerned. Paul begins the "grounding" of his thesis by indicating, first of all, how baptism establishes an involvement for the Christian in the death and resurrection of Christ (vv. 3-4). Then follow two parallel sequences (vv. 5-7 and 8-10 respectively). In each of these there is mention of the passage from death to resurrection (v. 5, v. 8), followed by an insistence upon the implications of this passage that must be recognized (cf. "we know," v. 6, v. 9) as far as freedom from the power of sin is concerned (v. 7, v. 10). The second sequence is more particularly focused upon Christ. Finally, the conclusion is drawn — first in general terms in v. 11, then more explicitly with respect to moral life in vv. 12-14.

In his opening assertion about baptism (vv. 3-4) Paul makes quite clear that the union with Christ established by the sacrament is not static but implies a dynamic insertion into what might be called the entire "career" of Christ. Christians have been baptized "into" the death of Christ. They have gone with him into the tomb (v. 4). They cherish the hope of following the pattern right through to resurrection. But this still lies in the future (cf. the future references in vv. 5, 8). Meanwhile baptism locates them somewhere "between" death and resurrection. The important thing is that it cuts them off completely from the old sinful existence and points them firmly in the direction of the new risen life (v. 4). As far as the old servitude to sin goes, they are "dead." They are not, of course, physically dead, nor is Paul introducing a new concept of "death" here. It is solely with respect to sin and its claims to dominion (chap. 5) that they are dead. The basis of this is that once a person has died no claims concerning moral life can be entered any more (v. 7; v. 10 [Christ]).

Paul is here continuing his image of sin as a "power." It is not that sin has been entirely destroyed. But Christians have been removed from its clutches because their baptismal involvement with the death of Christ has enabled them to become "dead" as far as it is concerned. It is a force that no longer has any hold over them. Or rather — since Paul's indicative really constitutes an imperative — it *ought* not have any hold upon them.

"Living to God"

Thus the negative theme — "dead to sin" — of v. 2b has been established. What about the positive direction in which baptism points Christians? What is the "newness of life" in which they are now to "walk" (v. 4)? While a bodily share in the risen life of the Lord must await their own resurrection, the union of Christians with Christ impels them towards the pattern of the risen life he now leads. Paul characterizes this very briefly as a "living to God."

Behind this simple phrase lies a rich theology suggestive of the total openness of Christ's whole existence to God. This encompasses not merely the obedience and fidelity of his earthly life (cf. 5:19; Phil 2:8), but continues into his risen existence as well (cf. Phil 2:11: "...it is to the glory of God the Father that Jesus Christ is Lord"; cf. 1 Cor 15:24, 28). It is by this continuing obedience that Jesus correctly and successfully replays the role of Adam, "subduing" the universe to the glory of God and enabling God's original design for the human race to find fulfilment. Though not sharing fully the risen life of the Lord, Christians, by virtue of their new life "in" Christ, are to give themselves over wholly to this attitude which spans his entire "career." In the words of Paul's conclusion in v. 11, they are to "consider" themselves "dead" as far as sin is concerned and "living to God" in Christ Jesus (v. 11).

Paul's new ethic rests, then, on a basis that is utterly christological. It comes down simply to a continued living out of the "obedience" of Christ, or, more accurately perhaps, it means Christians allowing Christ to live out in them his continuing obedience and fidelity to the Father (cf. Gal 2:19-20: "I through the law died to the law, in order that I might live to God. With Christ I hang upon the cross. I live now, not 'I,' but Christ lives in me"). United with Christ in this way, Christians can enter upon a new "service." Cut off from the old servitude to sin, they can become, as Christ was and is, wholly the instruments of the transforming righteousness of God. This Paul exhorts them to become by offering "their members" as "instruments" (or "weapons") of righteousness (vv. 13-14).

Paul's language here ("mortal body," "members") serves to make the point that, unlike Christ, Christians are still bodily anchored in the old world. It is in that world and nowhere else for the time being that this service of righteousness has to take place, just as Christ's obedience was once lived out bodily in the world. In fact, their bodily obedience constitutes the earthly expression of his continuing obedience to the Father. United with him in his obedience they, like him, embody in the world the fidelity and saving justice of God, they "*become* in him the righteousness of God" (2 Cor 5:21).

B. The New Obedience to Justice
6:15-23

Introduction
[15]What then? Shall we continue in sin since we are not under the rule of the law but under that of grace? God forbid!

Sequence 1: The New Obedience
[16]Do you not know that when you place yourselves in a situation of service with its implied obedience you make yourselves slaves to whomsoever you have subjected your-selves — in this case either slaves to sin, which leads to death, or slaves to obedience, leading to righteousness? [17]Thanks be to God — because you were once slaves of sin, but you have submitted from the heart to the pattern of teaching to which you were handed over [18]and, set free from sin, you have become slaves of righteousness.

Explanation
[19a]I use an example from human life to help you in your human weakness to understand.

Sequence 2: The Fruits
[19b]For as once you offered your members as slaves to uncleanness and lawlessness, with moral anarchy the result, so now offer your members as slaves to righteousness so that sanctification may result. [20]For when you were slaves of sin you were quite free as far as righteousness was con-cerned [21]and you know what return you had from that — things of which you are now ashamed! and the end of them is death. [22]But now, set free from sin and having become instead slaves of God, the return you get is sanctification and the end of that is eternal life. [23]For the wages of sin is death, whereas the gracious gift of God is eternal life in Christ Jesus our Lord.

A similar objection (v. 15) to the one at the beginning of the chapter launches Paul into a second treatment of the new obedience. Here the objection focuses more precisely upon the removal of the law. In the long run, as we have already noted, the removal of the law is for Paul the solution rather than the problem. But for the moment Paul delays to show how liberation from the law does not imply "lawlessness" or moral anarchy. On the contrary, the new life of Christians, no less than the old, involves an "obedience." The difference is that now it is an obedience leading to life, rather than one that leads to death.

To make this point Paul develops the idea, introduced in vv. 12-13, of offering oneself for service — to sin and righteousness respectively. He uses the image of a transfer from one form of service to another. After the introductory objection (v. 15), two parallel statements of the image follow (vv. 16-18; 19b-23), separated by something of an apology for the kind of image being used (v. 19a).

The sentence in which Paul establishes his image (v. 16) is one of the most compressed and contorted that he ever wrote. Almost as soon as he has begun it, Paul seems to realize that the image is going to run into difficulties and moves out of it into direct description of the situation to which it is meant to apply. His basic point seems to be that servitude of any kind involves an obedience. What has happened to Christians is that they have passed from one servitude and obedience to another. They have not simply passed out of obedience into a moral vacuum. Having left the service of sin, they have entered a new service or slavery to righteousness.

The idea of "slavery" hardly provides a congenial image for Christian moral life (we have noted that Paul does in fact offer an apology for it in v. 19). Certainly, it contrasts markedly with Paul's usual insistence upon freedom in connection with life in Christ. The image is rendered somewhat richer in its second phase (vv. 19b-23) by the concentration upon the *direction* in which the service points. Paul contrasts the two forms of service — the old and the new — in terms of the "return" or "fruits" which each, respectively, brings. The two sequences can be set out as follows:

Slavery to	Present Effects	Ultimate Consequences (Fruit)
Old: Sin (Lawlessness)	Uncleanness	Death
New: Righteousness	Sanctification	Eternal Life.

Paul continues here the point he has been making in chap. 5 that sin leads inevitably to death. Within his overall image he can speak ultimately of "Sin" as master paying death as "wages" (slaves received some kind of wage in the Greco-Roman world).

On the positive side, the service of righteousness (or simply "God," v. 22) leads, firstly, to "sanctification." This word certainly indicates moral transformation. But it carries also the overtones of the biblical idea of "holiness": bearing the stamp of close association with God. The sense is, then, that the lives of those who surrender themselves to the service of righteousness come more and more to display before the world the marks of God's ownership and claim. The end result on the positive side is "eternal life." Here there is no mention of "wages" — such language could re-introduce the sense of earned reward. Instead, Paul speaks of the eternal life as the "gracious gift" (*charisma*) of God. Grace remains the beginning and end of all.

C. Set Free from the Law for a Fruitful Union with Christ
7:1-6

Introduction
[1]Surely you must know, my brothers — for I speak to those who are familiar with the law — that the law has authority over a person only so long as that person is alive.

Marital Image
[2]Thus a married woman is bound by law to her husband as long as he lives. But if her husband dies she is free from the law that bound her to the husband. [3]Accordingly, if she gives herself to another man while the husband is still alive, she will be taken for an adulteress. But if the husband has

died, she will be free from that law and so will not be an adulteress if she gives herself to another man.

Application
⁴The conclusion from this, my brothers, is that you also have been put to death as far as the law is concerned through the body of Christ so that you might be joined to another, the One who has been raised from the dead, in order that our lives might bear fruit for God.

Old Existence
⁵For when we were in the flesh our sinful passions, provoked by the law, were at work in our members to make us fruitful only for death.

New Existence
⁶But now we have been removed from the law, having died to that which held us bound, so that we might render service in a new life under the influence of the Spirit, in place of the old existence controlled by the letter of the law.

Paul has been insisting upon the necessity of a right moral life for Christians. The present passage continues this theme, but with greater attention to the possibility rather than the necessity of such a life. The basis of this new possibility is the fact that Christians have been radically removed from the rule of the law and placed within a new sphere of influence — that of the Spirit. The passage is not, then, simply about freedom from the law. Paul goes further to insist that because of this freedom from the law Christians are also free from sin and so can (and must) live out the new moral capacity that has been created for them. The structure reflects this dual concern. With the aid of an image from marriage law Paul first establishes the fact that Christians are free from the law (vv. 2-4). He then outlines the new moral possibility, in contrast to the old captivity in sin, that this freedom creates (vv. 5-6).

The starting-point of the argument is the principle (formulated in v. 1b) that the law (or any law for that matter) can only apply to a person as long as that person lives. Death means release from the law and its claims. The image taken from marriage law illustrates this principle. The death of a spouse breaks the legal marriage bond and leaves the surviving partner free to contract a new union. Within the image as applied to the Christian situation, the married woman would represent the Christian, her first husband would be the law and the new husband she is subsequently free to marry would be Christ ("the one who has been raised from the dead," v 4). Schematically, the situation can be set out as follows:

Married Woman (= the Christian)----1st Husband (= the law)

~ ~ ~ ~(dies)

~ ~ ~ ~2nd Husband (= Christ)

Within the framework of the image the woman's freedom to contract the new union comes about through the death of the first husband. Applied strictly to the Christian situation, this would imply that it is the law which dies, whereas v. 4 makes quite clear that the "death" is not that of the law but of the Christian. Paul, however, does not envisage so strict a correspondence between image and reality. The image serves him to make the single point that it is through a *death* that freedom has been gained.

The Body of Christ

The "death" with respect to the law that Paul means here is clearly the "death" undergone in baptism, as outlined early in chap. 6. In v. 4 Paul further characterizes this "death" as having come about "through the body of Christ." This phrase is normally understood as referring to the physical body of Christ which suffered death on the cross and this may well be the primary meaning. However, "body" (*sôma*) is a rich concept in the Pauline literature. In contrast to "flesh" (*sarx*) the "body" for Paul is capable of resurrection. Moreover, besides referring to the physical body, *sôma* brings with it a wide range of meaning center-

ing around the idea of "communication."[1] In this wider
sense the *sôma* is that whereby one is "in touch" with the
world of persons and events, both to give and receive
impressions. In view of the emphasis in chap. 6 upon the
union with Christ established in baptism, it is highly likely
that the phrase "through the body of Christ" in v. 4 carries
this wider sense of "association" or "connection" with
Christ.

Thus when he writes, "you have been put to death to the
law through the body of Christ so that you might be joined
to another, the one who has been raised from the
dead, . . .," Paul probably has in mind that whole pattern
of association (= "body") with Adam, as outlined in chap.
5. The intimate association with Christ forged by baptism
allows one to be "dead" as far as the law is concerned and
so free from both its condemnation and its effects. On the
more positive side, it also means one is free for and actually
living a new union with the Risen Lord.

Pursuing the marital image in a rather attractive way,
Paul sees the new obedience as constituting the "offspring"
of this fruitful union between the Christian and the Risen
Lord. The parallel statements in vv. 5-6 show how this
"bearing fruit for God" contrasts sharply with the old
union under the law when there was a "bearing fruit for
death." In the description of the former situation given in v.
5 we meet once more Paul's principle that the law, far from
being a restraint on sin, actually fosters its growth. It is
precisely removal from the influence of the law that creates
the possibility of obedience and so leads to life.

How the law has this unhappy function and how, nonetheless, it fits into the divine scheme of things is something
Paul is going to have to explain and will in fact explain
forthwith. In fact, what is said about the negative role of
the law in v. 5 constitutes almost a thematic statement of
the treatment of the law to be given in 7:7-25. Similarly, the

---

[1]For further discussion of this aspect of "body" in Paul see B.J. Byrne, "Sinning
against One's Own Body: Paul's Understanding of the Sexual Relationship in 1 Cor
6:18," *Catholic Biblical Quarterly* 45 (1983) 608-16, esp. 610-12.

positive statement about the freedom for service in a new life under the influence of the Spirit anticipates the presentation of life in the Spirit given in 8:1-13. The details of vv. 5-6 receive their best commentary in the context of those subsequent passages, where Paul completes his discussion of the necessity and possibility of the new obedience.

REFLECTION

In these passages Paul has drawn up a basis for ethics in a milieu of grace. He has excluded moral anarchy without re-erecting a "works-reward" system of justification, which would bring back the destructive mercenary relationship to God. He has done this by placing the ethic for the "in-between" time upon a totally christological base. The possibility of obedience comes about through the freedom from sin and law created by the baptismal union with Christ. Good works are the "offspring" of a fruitful marriage between the believer and the Risen Lord. Such a conception preserves the "grace" and "gift" aspect of the new moral life. It gathers up the human contribution into the scope of the divine creativity, while at the same time it respects the inner connection between Christian behavior here and now and the life that flows as its "fruits."

Christians make that life-giving contribution in so far as they allow the risen Lord to imprint the living pattern of his obedient career upon their lives. They place their "bodies" at the service of God's righteousness in the world. Following the pattern of Christ, such an embodiment will attract the hostility of the forces of sin. It will involve bearing in one's mortal body the marks of the cross (2 Cor 4:10; Gal 6:17).

At the highest extreme, the baptismal consecration finds in martyrdom its most complete expression. But the martyr, who follows Christ in faith and obedience at the cost of death, in no way rejects the world. On the contrary the martyr humanizes the world and seeks to set it free for life by becoming wholly given up to the saving and ultimately victorious fidelity of God. Only in the context of embodying God's saving justice is Christian death "swallowed up in victory" (1 Cor 15:54). Oscar Romero lives on, as he said, in the Salvadoran people and becomes in death a more potent force for liberation.

READING:

*J.C. Beker, *Paul the Apostle* (Philadelphia: Fortress, 1980) 272-78.

*B.J. Byrne, "Living out the Righteousness of God: The Contribution of Rom 6:1 - 8:13 to an Understanding of Paul's Ethical Presuppositions," *Catholic Biblical Quarterly* 43 (1981) 557-81.

V.P. Furnish, *Theology and Ethics in Paul* (Nashville: Abingdon, 1968) 153-57, 171-87, 194-98.

E. Käsemann, "On Paul's Anthropology, in *Perspectives on Paul* (Philadelphia: Fortress, 1971; London: SCM) 1-31, esp. 21-23.

E. Schweizer, "Dying and Rising with Christ," *New Testament Studies* 14 (1967-68) 1-14.

R.C. Tannehill, *Dying and Rising with Christ: A Study of Pauline Theology* (Berlin: Töpelmann, 1967) 7-46.

W. Thüsing, *Per Christum in Deum* (2nd ed., Münster: Aschendorff, 1969) 67-101.

9

Life Under the Law — the Ethical "Impossibility" 7:7-25

Several times in the course of our path through Romans we have found Paul tossing off highly provocative statements about the negative effects of the law. It began with a simple comment in 3:20: ". . ., through the law comes (only) experience of sin." Then in 4:15: "For the law brings about wrath. Where there is no law neither is there transgression." In chap. 5: "sin is not booked up in the absence of law" (v 13); "The law came in only to multiply the trespass" (v. 20). In chap. 6 Paul points to the absence of law as the chief factor in the removal of Christians from the power of sin (cf. v. 14). Finally, we have just noted the far more explicit and quasi-thematic statement in 7:5 to the effect that the law stirs up sinful passions in our members to make them "fruitful for death."

Granted that the law was given by God, granted that Paul has already claimed to be "upholding" it (3:31) and granted, finally, that Romans is meant to be in large part a "dialogue with Judaism," it is intolerable that Paul should postpone any longer an explanation or justification of what he has been saying about the law. So he now sets out to explain how the law, though "holy" and "good" in itself, actually serves to hinder obedience rather than to foster it. Nonetheless, he will insist, even this hindrance of obedience or actual "provocation" of sin does have a part to play in the divine purpose.

What Paul says here about the law may have the appearance of being tied to a particular and narrow controversy of his own time, having little bearing upon wider concerns. But Paul's treatment of the law does have an abiding relevance. By "law" in Romans he does have in mind the (Jewish) law of Moses. But what he says about the uselessness, or rather the peril of addressing that particular legal code to a human situation where the root problem of sin has not been attended to is valid for all attempts to apply an external system of values or legal code where the same situation prevails. What Paul is about in Romans 7 is a subtle attempt to nail the problem of human sinfulness and destructiveness at its central core. He aims to show the impossibility of any remedy coming from purely human striving after goodness. In so doing he paves the way for his subsequent (chap. 8) indication of the Spirit as the only valid source of freedom and moral creativity.

The treatment of the law comes in two sections. The first (vv. 7-13) describes the encounter with the law in the form of a quasi-historical narrative set in the past. The second (vv. 14-25), in the present tense, describes that same encounter "from inside," as an experience. Throughout both sections Paul speaks in the first person singular and this has historically given rise to speculation as to whether the accounts may not record his own experience of life under the law. For a variety of reasons the view that Paul is speaking "autobiographically" has mostly lost currency. It is difficult to relate the struggle he describes to the normal religious formation of a young Jew. Nor does it agree with the report he gives in Phil. 3:4-6 concerning his own practice of the law ("as to righteousness under the law blameless," v. 6b). Rather, the "I" who speaks here is "Everyman" or, to be more precise, Paul adopts the situation and voice of every person confronted with the law or with external moral demand and left to his or her own resources. A somewhat more vexed question, and one that applies particularly to the second section, has to do with whether Paul is describing the moral dilemma of a person prior to conversion to Christianity or whether the struggle he outlines is one that is applicable strictly to the Christian life. We shall consider this issue when studying that later section.

A. The Encounter with the Law
7:7-13

Introduction
[7a]"What, then, shall we say? That the law is sin? God forbid!

Exposition
[7b]But I would not have known sin except through the law and I would not have known desire, if the law had not said, *You must not desire.* [8]But sin, seizing its opportunity, by means of the commandment, worked in me all manner of desire. For apart from the law sin is dead.

Narrative
[9]I was alive once, apart from the law. But when the commandment came, sin sprang to life. [10]I died and the commandment, which promised life, turned out to be death for me. [11]For sin, seizing its opportunity through the commandment, deceived me and through it killed me.

Conclusion
[12]So the law is holy and the commandment is holy, just and good. [13]Did what is good, then, prove to be death for me? God forbid! But sin, so that it might be shown to be sin, through this good thing was working death for me — that is, so that through the commandment sin might become sinful beyond measure.

Paul's treatment of the law has as its starting point the suggestion that the law is really identical with sin — a not unreasonable conclusion, granted the severity of his strictures upon its effects. Paul rebuts the objection in his characteristic manner. He then embarks upon a narrative designed to subtly distinguish the law from sin, while at the same time preserving the tenet he has been insisting upon all along —that it is the law which actually facilitates sin's appearance and coming to power.

The narrative, told in the first person singular, contains echoes of the "Fall" story in Genesis 2-3 (cf. esp. v. 11). The unnamed "I" who tells the sad tale is, then, in the first instance Adam. The patriarch was not, of course, confronted by the whole complex of the law of Moses. But in that he was presented with a specific positive command (more accurately, prohibition) he can stand for Paul as a type of every person confronted by the law or any external moral demand. The unidentified first-person style is presumably meant to serve as an invitation to all to read here something of their own personal history of sin.

The specific commandment cited in the narrative (v. 7) is not actually that of Gen 2:17 but a truncated form of the prohibition against "coveting" occurring in the Decalogue (Exod 20:17; Deut 5:21): literally, "You must not desire." The "desire" in question is not primarily sensual desire, certainly not in the restricted sense of sexual passion. There is evidence that the rabbis saw the entire law summed up in this single prohibition and Paul himself may view it in similarly comprehensive terms. What it forbids is the desire for independence and autonomy that rebels against the whole idea of human obedience to God. In this sense it stands for what Paul would regard as the core and essence of sin — the refusal to acknowledge God as God and oneself as human.

Paul evidently considers that such a "desire" or at least the possibility of its springing to life was (and is) part of the human condition. "Sin" in this sense was always "around." But, in the absence of the law, it was dormant, "dead" (v. 8b). It was the arrival of the law, in the form of the "commandment," that gave sin its opportunity, caused it to spring to life and work its fatal purpose.

How precisely did the coming of the commandment bring about this effect? It is clear from Romans 5 (especially vv. 14, 20) that Paul distinguishes sin (*hamartia*) or wrong-doing in general and "transgression" (*paraptōma, parakoē parabasis*). "Transgression" refers to the committing of some deed that is specifically excluded by the law and so formally qualified as being contrary to God's will. It adds to sin or wrongdoing the note of conscious rebellion against God. For Paul the law comes in to "multiply the trespass" (5:20) in the sense that it both lets human beings know that what they are contemplating is directly against God's will and at the same time provokes the very rebelliousness and "desire" (v. 7) for autonomy it aims to exclude. In this sense the commandment causes the hitherto quasi-dormant sinful impulse to "spring to life" and greatly increases the offense.

A Parable

At the risk of over-simplification, the following scenario might serve to illustrate Paul's point. Not far from a sizeable coastal town lies a secluded beach. No one swims there because prevailing off-shore currents make it dangerous. However, in summer it comes to be a place where young people from the town gather to sunbathe, play music and so forth. Though there is no evidence that they are using the beach for swimming, a group of over-conscientious citizens, noting that the young people are gathering there, feel con-strained to petition the municipality to erect a large notice on the cliff, warning of the danger and prohibiting swim-ming. So one weekend the young people find themselves confronted by a large, unattractive sign, forbidding some-thing that they had no intention of doing in the first place. For the first time they enter the water, defying both the danger and what they see as the unwarranted interference. The "commandment" in the form of the notice has (under-standably) provoked an instinct to rebel, hitherto dormant.

Paul seems to envisage that in similar fashion the com-mandment which promised life to Adam (at least by indicating how life was not to be forfeited) turned out to be his downfall. Sin used the (otherwise good and salvific) commandment to provoke the latent instinct for rebellion and so render it an instrument of death. "Sin" is, again, portrayed in personal terms and within the framework of the Genesis 3 story seems to play the role of the deceiving serpent (cf. v. 11). But Paul does not really think of it as a force external to human beings, even if, as chap. 5 suggests, it has an ambiance transcending purely individual sin. Sin remains that deep-seated, fundamental proneness in human beings to snatch at life by asserting independence over against God. The presence of the "commandment" or law in general provokes this latent tendency to full, domineering virulence, the end result of which is death.

Paul speaks here of death no doubt with reference to his general principle linking human mortality with sin (chap. 5). A peculiarity here, however, is the way he has the narrating "I" speak of death in the past tense: "I died" (v. 10), sin "killed me" (v. 11). Beyond the general linkage between sin and death, this language suggests a kind of anticipatory death of the "Ego" as a free, independent subject, capable of genuine control over his or her life. Sin, in coming to power, has knocked human beings out of the driving seat of their lives; it has usurped the wheel so as to convey them to death. The section to follow will describe this de-personalizing effect of sin from the "inside," as an experience.

So Paul, using this narrative of Adam's encounter with the commandment, has driven a wedge between the law and sin. He has shown how the law remains in itself "holy and just and good" (v. 12), even if it becomes, because of human nature, an instrument of sin and death. There remains only the question of why this good and holy law was allowed to fall into so fatal a role, seemingly contrary to its original purpose. Though Paul does not mention God explicitly, the final clauses in v. 13 allude to the divine purpose. They show how the nefarious dealing of sin with respect to the law was swept up into and ultimately made to serve the wider purpose of God. God used the law to "exorcise" sin out of the depths of human beings. He allowed the law to provoke rebellion, precisely so that what was hidden and latent might "appear" for what it was, be brought to the surface where it could be unmasked and dealt with effectively once and for all.

In short, God used the law much as a counsellor, suspecting that a client's life is being largely controlled by a hidden, subconscious anger of which the person is completely unaware, might seek to provoke that anger, bring it to the surface, where it can be recognized for what it is and dealt with effectively. Such a procedure will doubtless involve some ugly scenes. But the bringing up of the anger to consciousness will be an essential part of setting that person free.

So in this first part of his "apologia for the law" Paul has established the following. 1. The law is not identical with sin — in itself it is holy, just and good; its origins with God can be maintained. 2. It does have a genuine role, albeit a negative one, in the scope of salvation. Because of human weakness and proneness to sin it can never be a direct instrument leading to life; on the contrary, it points towards death. Nonetheless, on a kind of *felix culpa* basis, its negative working facilitates God's purpose to offer salvation by grace to those who feel and own their sin, who come to admit in faith their need for acceptance by a God who "justifies the ungodly."

B. Life Under the Law — The Fatal Tension 7:14-25

Introduction
14The law, as we well know, is spiritual. But I am fleshly, sold into slavery under sin.

Dilemma 1
15My own behavior I cannot understand. For it is not what I want to do that I do. But I do what I hate. 16If what I do is contrary to my will, this means that I agree with the law, and hold it to be admirable. 17But the situation is that it is no longer I who do this but the power of sin dwelling within me.

Dilemma 2
[18]For I am aware that in me, that is, in my flesh, there dwells nothing good. The will to do good is there, but the power to achieve it is not. [19]For I do not do the good I want to do, but the evil that I do not want, that I do. [20]But if what I do not want, that I do, then it is no longer I who do it but the power of sin dwelling within me.

Dilemma 3
[21]So I find that it is invariably the case that when I want to do what is right, evil lies close at hand. [22]I am in complete agreement with God's law according to my inmost self. [23]But I see another law in my members fighting against the law of my reasonable self and holding me captive to the law of sin, which dwells in my members.

Conclusion
[24]Wretched man that I am! Who will deliver me from this body of death? [25]God alone, thanks be to him, through Jesus Christ, our Lord. For left to my own resources, with my mind I serve the law of God, but in the flesh it is the law of sin that I serve.

With this text we enter upon one of the most celebrated and arresting passages of Romans. Describing the encounter with the law from the "inside," Paul vividly portrays the plight of the person who owns its reasonableness but cannot find the resources to fulfil it. In so doing he has composed a classic account of the age-old human dilemma summed up in the famous words of Ovid: *Video meliora proboque; deteriora sequor.*[1] In contrast to the terseness of the Roman poet, however, Paul builds up his effect by constant repetition of the basic plight. A structure is not immediately discernible. However, if v. 14 is taken as a kind of thematic introduction, then the description of the struggle is depicted in three "waves": vv. 15-17; vv. 18-20; vv. 21-23. It will be noted that the first and second of these sections conclude

---

[1]"I see the better way and I approve it. But I follow the worse," (*Metamorphoses* 7:19-21).

with the same phrase: "it is no longer I who do it but the power of sin dwelling within me." The third section outlines the tension in a slightly different way — that of the two "laws" seen to be struggling for moral supremacy within the person. The whole builds up to the climactic cry and response in vv. 24-25.

Since the argument is so repetitive, to work through it in detail would be both otiose and unnecessary. More important is an appreciation of the way Paul envisages the tension in the light of his particular view of the human person. This will involve some consideration of terms such as "flesh," "spirit," "mind" — necessary not just for this passage, but for all that is to follow in chap. 8.

"Flesh"

"Flesh" (*sarx*) is not simply equivalent to "body" in our sense, that is, as indicating the material part of human make-up, in contrast to the spiritual. Paul's understanding of "flesh" stems from the Old Testament and, rather than indicating a part or element of human nature, denotes the *whole person* from a particular aspect: the aspect of frailty, mortality, proneness to sin, hostility to God — all that makes for the merely human in contrast and to some extent opposition to God. While "flesh" at times comes very close to sin, Paul does not identify the two. It is in the flesh that sin gets its base of operations in human nature. If sin gets this hold, then indeed one is not merely "in" the flesh, but compelled to live "*according* to the flesh," "sold into slavery under sin" (v. 14b). But one can be "in the flesh" and not necessarily captive to sin. All pre-resurrection human existence must be existence "in" the flesh. But it need not be existence "according to the flesh," that is, dominated by sin. The distinction is crucial to an understanding of Paul's argument in Romans 7-8.

"Spirit"

Over against "flesh" stands "spirit" (*pneuma*). When speaking of *pneuma* Paul normally means the Holy Spirit —the active, life-giving power of God, especially associated with the influence of the Risen Christ. In extension from this usage *pneuma* can denote the atmosphere or sphere of power created by the Spirit in which Christian life is lived, energized and determined. In this way one is encouraged to live "according to the spirit." But Paul does use *pneuma* also in an anthropological way to denote an aspect of the human person — the human person as open to God, receptive of (eternal) life, being transformed into the likeness to God that represents the pinnacle of truly human growth and dignity. It is to the human being *qua* "spirit" that the Holy Spirit has particular access. The Spirit works to bring this aspect to dominance.

"Mind"

"Spirit" in this sense does not feature in the passage under consideration — a fact that is significant for its overall interpretation, as we shall see. There is only the opening reference to the law as "spiritual" (*pneumatikos*) — an allusion, it would seem, to its original, but unavailing purpose to give (eternal) life (cf. v. 9). What corresponds to "flesh" here on the more positive side is "mind" (*nous*, vv. 23, 25), also referred to as the "inner man" (v. 22). "Mind," again, describes the whole person — this time under the aspect of a knowing, reasoning and judging being, with a certain element of "will" or aspiration included.

The Fatal Tension

With an understanding of these terms we can better approach Paul's depiction of the human plight in the present passage. The "I" here cries out of a human situation which is not merely "in" the flesh but, as v. 14 makes clear, in the flesh "sold under sin." When confronted by the law, the "spiritual" law that promises life, "I" really go out to it, acknowledge that it is "admirable" (v. 16) and conceive a real yearning to fulfil it and so obtain life. In terms of the third sequence, I consent to it according to the "inner man" (v. 22), "in my mind" (vv. 23, 25). But "sin," which has its controlling hold over me in the flesh tugs powerfully in the opposite direction. It uses the presence of the law to stir up the hostility and rebellion latent in the flesh. Thus it renders me incapable of doing the good that I want and compels me to do the evil that (in my "mind") I detest.

In a way that seems to correspond to the "death" of the Ego in the preceding passage (vv. 9, 10), it is no longer "I" that is in control but "sin dwelling within me" (vv. 17, 20). An unbearable tension is set up within me. I witness an unequal struggle going on "in my members" (that is, my "fleshly" existence considered in various particular situations). Through the dominance of sin I sense myself being dragged into moral failure and set inescapably in the direction of death. The situation might be depicted like this:

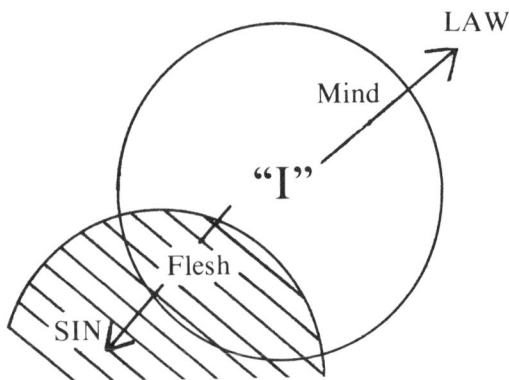

The problem is, of course, that the law, for all its good intention, remains something external. It can only exhort, threaten punishment, ultimately condemn. It cannot address the root problem, which is internal: sin in the flesh. It serves only to provoke rebellion and so to foster rather than hinder the designs of sin. Confronted with the law, then, human beings can do nothing: "Wretched *man* that I am!" They must turn to other than human resources for deliverance: "Who will deliver me from this body of death?" (v. 24) — that is, from this whole "bind" or situation of death. The answer can only be "God" — God acting through Jesus Christ (v. 25a).

"Christian" or "Pre-Christian" Experience?

Many Christians throughout the centuries, following Augustine and Luther, have found in this passage a reflection and resonance of their own moral struggle. It is unlikely, however, that Paul understands the dilemma he depicts here to be something characteristic of Christian life, that is, as belonging to post- rather than pre-conversion experience. Some things, it is true, do favor such an interpretation. The account is told in the present tense. More tellingly, though it is a detail, there is the evidence of v. 25, where Paul after the triumphant response of thanks to God through Jesus Christ, that is, after this most "Christian" cry, continues on in v. 25b very much from within the former perspective of slavery to sin. This seems to suggest that the latter coexists within the Christian situation.

But it is not what is present but what is absent from this passage which is decisive. The absent factor is the Spirit — the power or atmosphere energizing Christian life in Paul's understanding. The absence of the Spirit from this passage contrasts sharply with its presence, indeed its dominance, in the one to follow (8:1-13). This contrast is absolutely central to Paul's argument in that, where Rom 7:14-25 presents the moral struggle without the Spirit, Rom 8:1-13 presents the same struggle where the Spirit, rather than sin, is the dominant force. To refer both passages indiscriminately to the Christian life blunts the contrast and renders ineffectual Paul's dramatic portrayal of God's intervention to release the Spirit in 8:1-4. Argument based on the use of the present tense (probably a dramatic device, used because

Paul is recounting experience rather than "history" as in vv. 7-13) or on the sequence in v. 25 cannot overthrow the basic consideration stemming from the absence of the Spirit, which points decisively to pre-conversion experience.

But to see the matter wholly in temporal categories, as a question simply of "before conversion" or "after conversion," is to fail to do full justice to Paul. The person he depicts in 7:14-25 is the person utterly reliant on his or her human resources, a human being unaided by God. The unequal struggle with sin issues in the desperate cry "*Who* will deliver me from this body of death?" and the response can only be: "God." Thus alongside the time contrast, and perhaps more fundamental, is a contrast between a human being struggling with sin unaided by God and a human being turning to God and ultimately helped by him (through the Spirit) in the same contest. V. 25b highlights this contrast in that, coming immediately after the cry to God, it vividly recalls again the impossible dilemma of the person in the first situation — I, "left to my own resources," going it alone apart from God. In the face of this situation of "moral impossibility," 8:1-4 will proclaim the "possibility" opened up for human beings through the "invasion" of the Spirit.

REFLECTION

With the contrast presented in this way, the passage under consideration retains its abiding relevance for the Christian situation. It shows the bankruptcy of any attempt to solve moral problems simply by the imposition of external law, where the root problem in human nature is not addressed. More deeply, it teaches the impossibility of overcoming the hold of sin through human resources alone. It challenges all solutions proceeding from a purely secular humanism, maintaining that solely in relationship to God can true liberation be found.

Doubtless Christians will continue to find that the struggle depicted here, its sense of guilt, even its despair, finds resonance in their lives. But rather than concluding that that is how things should be, that 7:14-25 describes the "normal" Christian situation, perhaps they should ask whether at that point they are not trying to "go it alone" apart from God in a way more suggestive of the "pre-conversion" rather than the "Christian" situation. The passage then becomes a supreme "test" of spirits — a challenge constantly to turn to the Spirit who alone creates the moral possibility that flows from within in a truly humanizing way.

READING:

*G. Bornkamm, "Sin, Law and Death. An Exegetical Study of Romans 7," in *Early Christian Experience* (New York: Harper & Row, 1969; London: SCM) 87-104.

*B.J. Byrne. "Living out the Righteousness of God," *Catholic Biblical Quarterly* 43 (1981) 557-81, esp. 565-70.

J.D.G. Dunn, "Rom 7, 14-25 in the Theology of Paul," *Theologische Zeitschrift* 31 (1975) 257-73.

J.A. Fitzmyer, "Paul and the Law," in *To Advance the Gospel* (New York: Crossroad, 1981) 186-201; simplified version in (M.J. Taylor, ed.) *A Companion to Paul* (New York: Alba House, 1975) 73-87.

W.G. Kümmel, *Man in the New Testament* (Philadelphia: Westminster, 1963) 50-61.

*C.L. Mitton, "Romans VII Reconsidered," *Expository Times* 65 (1953-54) 78-81, 99-103, 132-35.

*J.A.T. Robinson, *Wrestling with Romans* (London: SCM, 1979; Philadelphia: Fortress) 82-95.

*W.D. Stacey, *The Pauline View of Man* (London: Macmillan, 1956) 128-36 ("Spirit"), 154-73 ("Flesh"), 181-93 ("Body"), 198-205 ("Mind").

10

Life in the Spirit — the Ethical "Possibility"
8:1-13

A. The Freedom Created Through God's Act in Christ
8:1-4

Theme
[1]There is now no condemnation for those in Christ Jesus.
[2]For the law of the life-giving Spirit has set me free in
Christ Jesus from the law of death-dealing sin.

God's Act
[3]For what the law could not do, in that it was weak because
of the flesh, God himself has done: to deal with sin, he sent
his own Son in the likeness of flesh dominated by sin and
condemned sin there in the flesh, [4]in order that what the
law rightly required might be fulfilled in us, who walk now,
not according to the flesh, but according to the Spirit.

The opening verses of chap. 8 mark a breakthrough into
an atmosphere of freedom and life. Paul emerges from his
grim account of the helpless situation under the law to out-

line the new possibility opened up by the Spirit. His portrayal of the new possibility, however, explicitly responds to that
former situation, since the contrast between what is possible
to human beings "going it alone" and what is possible when
they surrender to God remains central to his argument. So
chap. 7 and the early part of chap. 8 are like two panels of
the one diptych. They must be read in close connection if
one is to appreciate the full force of Paul's proclamation in
chap. 8.

The crucial difference in the new situation is indicated at
the end of the first sentence: "in Christ Jesus." To be "in
Christ" means to have been radically cut off, through faith
and baptism, from the old, sin-dominated existence "in
Adam" and to be living now in a sphere or context of salvation constituted by the power of the Risen Lord. This power
of the Risen Lord is for Paul, as we have already noted, the
Spirit. Thus "those in Christ" are those who live in the
atmosphere of the Spirit and whose lives are thereby able to
be shaped by its liberating power. With the power of the
Spirit energizing their lives in this way, human beings are no
longer on their own, locked into an unequal struggle with
the power of sin (7:7-25), the outcome of which must be
"condemnation" (8:1). On the contrary, the Spirit now
brings them under the scope of God's power, where a right
moral life becomes a possibility and the threat of condemnation (because of sin) is lifted. Thus "there is now no (necessary) condemnation for those in Christ Jesus" (v. 1).

V. 2 describes the difference in terms of "law." The old law,
since it was simply an external indicator of God's will,
became an instrument of sin and so bound me into an impri-
sonment leading to death. "In Christ" it has been replaced by
the Spirit which functions as a liberating force for life. Inter-
estingly, Paul continues to speak of "law" (*nomos*) even with
reference to the Spirit. He does so presumably because for
him *nomos* retains the basic sense of that which indicates
God's will for the moral life of human beings. This role was
played (unsuccessfully) by the old (Mosaic) law. But the
Spirit, in that it creates the moral life of human beings, can
also be described in terms of "law." The difference is that

whereas the old law could only make its demands in an external way that did nothing to address the radical problem of sin in human nature, the Spirit has become a law "written in the heart." As such it really does address the problem and so can effect true moral liberation.

In the following two verses (3-4) Paul traces the origin of the new moral possibility right back to God's original act in Christ. Continuing his contrast between the impotence of merely human resources and the power of God, he first gives a summary of the old helplessness under the law (cf. 7:14-25): "What the law could not do, in that it was weak because of the flesh." To this incapacity of the law responds God's liberating action in Christ: to deal with sin, God sent his own Son in the "likeness" of flesh dominated by sin.

Much discussion has centered on the force of the word "likeness" (*homoiôma*) here. In early centuries the expression encouraged a Docetic view of the Incarnation (that is, one which sees the Son taking on the appearance but not the reality of human nature). It continues to be seen as something of a shield inserted by Paul to ward off too close a connection of Christ and sin. But Paul hardly has to defend the general Christian axiom that Christ "knew no sin" (2 Cor 5:21). "Likeness" probably serves, in fact, to strengthen rather than soften the identification of Christ with the human condition. What Paul wants to bring out is the paradox of God's costly involvement in the human situation. One so close to him as to be "his own Son" enters totally into the sin-dominated situation. In the language of Phil 2:6-7, he who was "in the form of God...emptied himself, taking the form of a slave, becoming in the likeness of men." It was in the flesh, that is, wholly from *within,* that Christ was able to achieve God's work of "condemning" sin once and for all. In contrast to the law, which had always remained simply an external code, provoking rebellion rather than quelling it, Christ entered fully into the "flesh" and there, fully within the human situation, struck at the core or root of the problem: "sin in the flesh."

V. 4 states the goal or consequence of the divine action in terms of the new ethical possibility it opens up for human

beings. "What the law rightly required," that is, the righteousness which the law as expression of the divine will
demanded but could not give the capacity to fulfil, that
righteousness is now "fulfilled in us, who walk now, not
according to the flesh, but according to the Spirit." All-
important here is the passive "be fulfilled." Paul does not
say "in order that we might fulfil," which might suggest
that, merely assisted by what God has done, we can now
embark upon a new (and successful) life of works. There is
indeed a fulfilment, but it is something which God, the
author of all, works in us through the Spirit as a consequence of the work of Christ. A new righteousness is
brought about. It is produced "in us" and in this sense truly
engages all our human capacity. But it remains fundamentally the gift and creation of God.

Thus, over against the impotence of any system of morality imposed purely from outside, Paul has traced the
possibility of moral renewal right back to what God has
done in Christ. In so doing he has provided a basis for
Christian ethics that is strikingly Trinitarian. All goes back
to the act of the *Father,* "sending his own *Son*," who in his
costly conquest of sin, releases the new moral capacity in
the shape of the *Spirit.*

Moreover, we have in the "sending" statement of vv. 3-4
something that complements the key summary of the gospel given in 3:21-26. Where that earlier statement saw the
work of Christ as the embodiment of God's saving fidelity
to the sinful world, the present statement views it more
particularly from the perspective of the new moral possibility it opens up. There is close connection between the two
in that what Paul is saying about the new righteousness
created and fulfilled "in" Christians through the Spirit
represents the continuation of the same saving fidelity of
God. Offering their bodies as instruments of righteousness
to God (6:13) Christians allow themselves in Christ, to be
built into the same fidelity. In this sense their lives represent a "living out" of the righteousness of God. His offer of
saving fidelity to the world continues in and through their

"bodies" — that is, through their (at times) costly association with that world.

A Parable

From the age of twelve Brett has proved an impossible boy to handle in the local high school. He flouts all rules, he is constantly thrown out of class as a disruptive influence. Now he is beginning to get into trouble with the law, breaking into houses, attempting to steal cars; there are serious acts of vandalism. The headmaster is at his wits' end in regard to Brett. Threats and the imposition of penalties —detention, suspension from class, and so forth — only seem to provoke worse rebellion. Nothing seems to be left save expulsion, with commitment to reform school sure to follow.

David, a young teacher at the school, has other ideas. Though he has not had any greater success in controlling Brett than other teachers, he knows a bit more about his history. He has learned that Brett's father left home when the boy was about eight, after years of drunken, violent assault on his mother, his younger sister and Brett himself. He suspects that deep within Brett lies a fearful trauma caused by years of suffering at the hands of a violent, totally unpredictable and terrifying parent. This has made it impossible for Brett to respond rationally to any authority system whether in the shape of school rules or civil law.

David begins to visit Brett's home. He gets a welcoming response from his increasingly desperate mother, but Brett himself is cool and suspicious. He does respond, however, to an invitation to some outings — going together to amusement parlors, to the trots, an occasional film; sometimes staying over for some days in David's apartment. Brett's behavior on these occasions is frequently bad. He slips away without a word, he wrecks David's record player, breaks into his car and tries to drive off. His language is foul. There are occasions of real physical violence. There is virtually no conversation, no communication for weeks on end.

But David perseveres. He knows he is being tested. One day they are sitting together in the car by the sea, eating fish and chips, watching the waves; there is a new sense of feeling comfortable in each other's presence. Brett makes a first move in talking about his background, his feelings and the conflicts he experiences. It is only a start. There are many more occasions of conflict and hurt for David. But gradually a language develops. It becomes possible to discuss values that might lead to a way of life less in conflict with his family, his school and society.

Eighteen months later Brett is still far from being fully at ease. He remains moody and suspicious. But he does his school work with some sense of purpose. He has not had a brush with the law for over a year. He respects other people's property and their rights to live undisturbed. Somehow, through the relationship with David, the values that the school regulations and the ordinary civil law enshrined, things which he violently rejected in their form as law, he has quietly absorbed. Gradually he is letting those values shape his life into a more peaceful and creative pattern. David has paid a heavy cost. But Brett in a real sense has been set in the direction of a fully human life.[1]

The parable's application to Romans 7-8 scarcely needs detailed elaboration. Before David took his cause in hand Brett was in a situation akin to human beings under the law. The deep-seated trauma left by his father's behavior corresponds to the situation of "sin in the flesh." The imposition of law as an external force, whether in the shape of school rules or policing did not address itself to the real problem but could only stir up worse rebellion. What David did in his fidelity as a teacher was to establish a relationship with Brett *before he changed.* In biblical language he "justified" him as "ungodly." He entered fully into the "flesh" of Brett's own situation, "got alongside him," as

---

[1]There is nothing unique about this story. It could doubtless be verified, with variations, in the experience of many teachers and social workers. In its present form it owes much to the account given by John Embling in his moving book: *Tom: A Child's Life Regained* (Harmondsworth: Penguin, 1978).

it were, paying a considerable cost for his sustained faith-fulness. Gradually a moral change took place. The values the external law really wanted to inculcate but could not bring about because the basic trauma was unhealed, Brett came to inwardly appropriate within the framework of the new relationship.

All examples limp. But this may serve to illustrate in some fashion the way in which Paul sees a new moral possibility in the shape of the Spirit flowing from the rela-tionship established by the costly fidelity of Christ. In tra-ditional theological language, "justification" issues forth in "sanctification." Christians are enabled "to render service in a new life under the influence of the Spirit, in place of the old existence controlled by the letter of the law" (Rom 7:6).

B. Life in the Spirit — The Creative Tension
8:5-13

Two Ways: Flesh & Spirit
[5]For those who live according to the flesh have their minds set on the things of the flesh, while those who live according to the Spirit have theirs set on the things of the Spirit. [6]Now what the flesh is really aiming at is death, whereas the aim of the Spirit is life and peace. [7]This is because the intent of the flesh is hostile to God. It does not submit to his law, nor can it (ever) do so. [8]Those who really live in the flesh cannot please God.

The Hope of Life through the New Righteousness
[9]But you are not living in the power of the flesh, but in that of the Spirit — that is, if the Spirit of God is really dwelling in you. For if someone lacks the Spirit of Christ, then that person does not really belong to him. [10]But if Christ dwells in you, then, though the body be mortal because of sin, the Spirit means life because of righteousness. [11]If the Spirit of the One who raised Jesus from the dead dwells in you, the One who raised Christ from the dead will give life also to

your mortal bodies through the power of the indwelling Spirit.

Concluding Exhortation
[12]So then, my brothers, we are people under obligation —not to the flesh, to live according to the flesh. [13]For if you live according to the flesh you are destined to die. But if in the Spirit you put to death the (base) deeds of the body, you will live.

The liberation God has brought about in Christ has created a new ethical possibility for human beings (vv. 3-4). But that possibility must be lived out. The fatal alternative — living according to the flesh — is still very much open and a choice must be made. So in vv. 5-8 Paul places side by side the two alternatives — living according to the flesh and living according to the Spirit — and indicates the consequences, death and life, that flow from each.

Treating of 7:14-25 we argued that the fatal tension there described should not be considered characteristic of the Christian situation. The present passage shows, however, that a certain tension is nonetheless part of Christian life. One has to live between the pull of the flesh and that of the Spirit (cf. also Gal 5:16-26). What, then, is the difference between the tension described here and the moral dilemma of chap. 7? In the new Christian situation it is possible to walk according to the flesh and reap the fatal consequences, death. It is *possible,* but it is not *necessary.* That is the crucial difference from the situation described in chap. 7. In the former situation the infestation of the flesh by sin, produced an irresistible necessity of following the flesh. "I" felt myself dragged helplessly to death. In the new atmosphere created by the Spirit Christians do indeed remain in some sense "in" the flesh, but they are not in the flesh in the sense of being wholly determined by it. They do not *have* to "walk according to the flesh."

REFLECTION

In this view of the Christian life as involving both tension and choice Paul would seem to be in agreement with the insights of modern psychology.[2] The kind of dilemma described in Chap. 7, where a resolution between aspiration, on the one hand, and capability, on the other, is unattainable, describes a situation where tension becomes unbearable and destructive, where it leads to elimination of the real "I" and ultimately to death. But the tension involved in the chap. 8 situation would seem to be the sort of constructive tension that makes for life and growth. The crucial difference, what Paul would see as the presence or absence of law, has to do with values — whether they are presented as part of an external, alien complex producing fear and guilt, or whether they are internally owned and constantly reaffirmed in free option for the Spirit.

Destiny to Life

In vv. 9-11 Paul spells out somewhat more explicitly the life-giving consequences of living in the Spirit. (He reverses the "indwelling" language: instead of Christians living in the Spirit, he speaks now of their allowing the Spirit [or "Christ," v. 10] to dwell within them. The two forms of expression seem to be quite interchangeable.) By allowing the Spirit to dwell within them in the sense of determining their moral life Christians live out their intimate belonging to Christ (v. 9) and so have a chance of sharing his destiny to resurrection. "If (through the Spirit) Christ dwells within you, then, though the body be mortal because of sin, the Spirit means life because of righteousness" (v. 10). That is, the Spirit does not remove the immediate destiny to physical death which is the consequence of human sin (chap. 5) — a destiny which Christ himself, though sinless, underwent in solidarity with sinners. But the Spirit introduces into human

---

[2]Cf., e.g., D. Capps, *Life Cycle Theory and Pastoral Care* (Philadelphia: Fortress, 1983) 20-22.

life that transforming righteousness which leads to resurrection.

In this way the link between righteousness and resurrection is maintained. Ultimately, however, all goes back to the fidelity of God. Christians do not attain resurrection by working at their own righteousness. Instead they accept God's gift of righteousness by allowing his Spirit to dwell within them and work its transforming effect. It is in view of this transformation that "the Spirit of the One who raised Christ from the dead will give life also to your mortal bodies through the power of the indwelling Spirit" (v. 11). That is, as God was faithful to the righteousness of Christ, raising him from the dead, so he will be faithful to the righteousness which he himself has created in Christians during their mortal existence.

Concluding Exhortation (8:12-13)

The entire "ethical excursus" begun at 6:1 is brought to a conclusion in vv. 12-13. Christians are people "under obligation." They are both free for and bound by a new obedience. If they choose to forego this obedience and live "according to the flesh" they are, quite simply, going to die. If they put to death the deeds of the body, they will live (v. 13). The "death" and "life" of which Paul is now speaking is clearly a living and dying that transcends ordinary physical mortality. "Death" is the falling out of God's hands that makes physical death simply final. "Life" now means the resurrection life that remains a hope even in the face of physical death.

In connection with "life" Paul speaks of "putting to death through the Spirit the deeds of the body." This language implies at first sight a rather pessimistic attitude to the physical body, an impression that could have been avoided by writing "deeds of the flesh" rather than "deeds of the body." But Paul may not be using "body" pejoratively. The choice of "body" suggests that the Spirit grants the capacity to see all present attachments (cf. the sense of *sôma* as medium of communication) to the world from the perspective of death and resurrection. In so far as these bodily involvements immerse Christians in the fallen, passing aspect of the world (the "present age" of Jewish apocalyptic) they can and must be allowed to die. But the "dying" that this involves retains also, through God's fidelity, the hope of resurrection. It is precisely this hope that gives value to bodily existence here and now (cf. 1 Cor 6:13-14). Paul's asceticism is intrinsically tied to resurrection hope.

REFLECTION

Paul has thus brought his great "ethical excursus" to a close by showing how the new obedience holds out the promise of life because of the fidelity of God. The God who was faithful to Jesus in his obedient faith will also be faithful to us, as we allow the Risen Lord to relive his obedience through the Spirit in our own lives. Christ's obedience "unto death" involved faith in a God who was faithful and powerful over death. Christian obedience likewise involves a continuing faith. If it is not always a faith exercised in the face of physical death, it is at least faith that must be exercised in the face of the daily "dying" which "putting to death the deeds of the body" involves.

In seeing that the obedience of the Christian life involves a continuing faith, we are not at all far here from the faith of Abraham in chap. 4. Abraham had to believe in a God who gave life to the dead (v. 17b). His faith was paradigmatic for Christians in that they too have to believe in a God who raised Jesus from the dead (vv. 23-25). What the present passage adds to this is the thought that Christian faith, as well as looking back to God's raising of Jesus, has, like Abraham's believing, to look forward as well. Central to the faith of Christians is the belief that the God who was faithful to Jesus in his obedient death will also be faithful to them as they live out their obedience in a situation of bodily mortality. Thus Jesus is paradigm in both his faith and his resurrection — something to which Paul gives striking expression in 2 Cor 4:13-14. With reference to the mortal risks and sufferings of the apostolic life, he writes: "Having the same spirit of faith, according to what Scripture says, 'I believed and therefore I spoke,' we too believe and therefore we speak, knowing that the One who raised the Lord Jesus will raise us also with Jesus and set us along with you."

READING:

B.J. Byrne, "Living out the Righteousness of God," *Catholic Biblical Quarterly* 43 (1981) 557-81, esp. 567-81.

M.D. Hooker, "Interchange in Christ," *Journal of Theological Studies* NS 22 (1971) 349-61, esp. 354-55.

*S. Lyonnet, "St. Paul: Liberty and Law," in (J.M. Oesterreicher, ed.) *The Bridge. A Yearbook of Judaeo-Christian Studies* 4 (1962) 229-51; simplified version: "Paul's Gospel of Freedom," in (M.J. Taylor, ed.) *A Companion to Paul* (New York: Alba House, 1975) 89-99.

——————, "Gratuité de la justification et gratuité du salut," *Studiorum paulinorum congressus internationalis catholicus* (2 Vols., Rome: Biblical Institute, 1963) 1.95-110.

P. von der Osten-Sacken, *Römer 8 als Beispiel paulinischer Soteriologie* (Göttingen: Vandenhoeck & Ruprecht, 1975) 226-44.

E. Schweizer, Art. "*huios, ktl*___," in (G. Kittel ed.) *Theological Dictionary of the New Testament* 8.374-76, 382-84.

11

The Hope of
Full Freedom and Glory
8:14-39

A. Sons and Heirs of God
8:14-17

Theme
¹⁴For all whose lives are shaped by the Spirit of God are sons of God.

Proof
¹⁵For it is not a spirit of slavery that you have received — something to drive you back again to fear. But you have received a spirit of sonship, in which we cry out, "Abba, Father." ¹⁶The Spirit himself in this way bears witness along with our spirit that we are God's children.

From Sons to Heirs
¹⁷And if we are children, then we are heirs as well — heirs of God, coheirs with Christ — provided we are prepared to suffer with him in order that we might also share his glory.

Paul has shown both the necessity for obedience in a milieu of grace and also its possibility because the law has been replaced by the Spirit. He has just (vv. 9-11) indicated how the obedience created by the Spirit is the basis for hope in the face of continuing mortality. This hope for eternal life or glory becomes once more the centre of attention and so at last, after the long ethical excursus, the proper theme of Romans 5-8 is resumed.

In v. 14 Paul pursues the theme of "hope" by picking up "will live" at the end of the preceding verse and developing it in terms of "sons (children) of God." The idea of "sonship" is introduced casually and without explanation. Paul does not appear to be coining a new metaphor for Christian life but applying to Christians a standard and well-known designation. It is going to feature prominently in his argument from here on (as it does also in somewhat parallel fashion in Galatians 3-4). What meaning does this language have?

References to Israel as "son(s)/children of God," while not particularly numerous, occur across a wide range of Old Testament literature (e.g., Exod 4:22-23; Deut 14:1; Is 1:2-4; Hos 1:10; 11:1; Wis 18:13). The status of sonship flows from election. It marks Israel off from all other nations in privileged closeness to God. God's "sons" are those whom he owns to be his people and whom he intends to favor. In the later Jewish literature "sonship" acquires a distinct eschatological tone. It describes the glorious Israel of the end-time, destined to inherit the eschatological blessings of salvation. These overtones attaching to the "sonship" language account for Paul's introduction of it at this point. By calling those whose lives are shaped by the Spirit "sons of God" Paul is designating them as members of the New Israel, destined to inherit the blessings of salvation — that is, as those who in the fullest sense "will live."

But the status of sonship requires some proof. To provide it Paul points to a further role played by the Spirit. Up till now he has spoken of the Spirit as the liberating and energizing force in Christian behavior. Now, in a way that echoes the "pouring out of God's love into our hearts" in 5:5, the Spirit is that which attests the new closeness to God. It gives empirical proof that we are sons by making us cry out, "Abba, Father," something which expresses a confidence and intimacy with God in marked contrast to the fear characteristic of the old slavery.

Neither here nor in the parallel passage in Gal 4:6 does Paul stop to explain this "Abba" cry in the Spirit. He seems to be alluding to a phenomenon well-known and characteristic of Christian experience, not confined to communities founded by himself. It is generally agreed that in this address — one of the rare instances where the New Testament records the original Aramaic — we have a historical preservation of Jesus' own distinctive address to the Father. In the Gospels it is found on the lips of Jesus only in Mark 14:35 — though that is a significant instance from a Pauline point of view, since the context is that of Jesus' agony in the garden before he goes in obedience and faith to his death. In the two Pauline instances (Rom 8:15 and Gal 4:6) the "Abba" cry is placed on the lips of Christians. But the impulse to address God in this intimate way comes from the Spirit (in Gal 4:6: "the Spirit of his Son"). Thus the sonship privilege which this cry attests is wholly christologically based. It is "in Christ" or "in his Spirit" that Christians are and know that they are "sons/children of God."

Inheritance

But the "Abba" address to God expresses something more than intimacy. In the Jewish context in particular, fatherhood connotes the passing-on of the family inheritance. Thus the address to God as "Abba" includes the hope that he will provide the eschatological inheritance that is promised. The shift, then, from "sons/children of God" to "heirs" (v. 17) is natural.

The "inheritance" language occurring here also evokes the promise to Abraham in chap. 4. In calling Christians "heirs of God" Paul is designating them as the intended beneficiaries of that promise of "inheriting the world" which God gave to Abraham "and to his seed." They are "seed of Abraham" because they follow his path of faith. But, as Gal 3:16 suggests more explicitly, it is solely in Christ that they are "seed"; they have no life of faith apart from him. Thus, while truly "heirs of God," they are properly "co-heirs of Christ" and as "co-heirs" they have to follow his pattern of entrance into inheritance. They must suffer with him in order to share his glory (v. 17b). The following passage now takes up the question of the relationship between suffering and glory in the context of Christian hope.

B. The Cosmic Hope of Liberation
8:18-30

Theme
[18]For I reckon that the sufferings of the present time are a small price to pay for the glory that is going to be revealed in us.

1. *Groaning of "Creation"*
[19]For creation waits with eager longing for the revealing of the sons of God. [20]For creation was subjected to futility not by its own will but on account of the one who was meant to subdue it. And so the hope remained [21]that the creation itself would be set free from its bondage to decay so as to share the freedom associated with the glory of the children of God. [22]For we know that the entire creation has been groaning together in the pangs of childbirth right up till the present.

2. *Groaning of "Ourselves"*
[23]Not only creation, but we too, having the first fruits of salvation in the shape of the Spirit, groan with respect to ourselves; we await full sonship, the redemption of our bodies. [24]For we are in a situation of salvation, but only in hope. Now a hope that is in sight is not really a hope at all. For who hopes for what is seen? [25]But if we go on hoping for what we do not see, then we await it with endurance.

3. *Groaning of the Spirit*

²⁶In the same way the Spirit comes to our aid in our weakness. For we do not know what it is right to pray for. But the Spirit himself intercedes for us with groans too deep for utterance. ²⁷And the Searcher of hearts knows what is the intention of the Spirit: that he intercedes for the saints in accordance with God's will for them.

The Plan of God

²⁸We know that in every way God works for the benefit of those who love him, those, that is, who have been called according to his purpose. ²⁹For those whom he chose beforehand, he preordained that they should become sharers in the image of his Son, so that he might become the firstborn among many brethren. ³⁰And those whom he preordained, these he also called, and those whom he called, these he also justified, and those whom he justified, these he has also glorified.

We have now reached that stage of Paul's treatment of Christian hope where he confronts head-on the question of suffering. V. 18 gives precise expression to what is to be the dominant theme: the incomparable richness of the "glory to be revealed" over against present sufferings. As we noted when dealing with the foreshadowing of this theme in chap. 5, "this present time" entails suffering because, in a way never envisaged in the simpler Jewish eschatology, there is an interim stage between justification and full salvation when Christians are buffeted in the body by the conditions of the present age. At this stage, when they are still so much bodily part of that suffering world, Christians must keep their eyes upon the hope that full salvation entails. It is a hope of arriving at the public revelation of that "glory," or likeness to God, which, according to the Jewish tradition, will represent the complete realization of God's eternal design for human beings and their world.

Paul's pursuit of this theme follows in four clearly defined stages. Quaint though it may sound at first sight, the first three stages are all characterized by a "groaning" motif and can be distinguished according to the subject of this "groaning." In vv. 19-22 "creation" groans; in vv. 23-25 "we" groan; and in vv. 26-27 there is reference to groans uttered by the Spirit. Vv. 28-30 form a conclusion where Paul summarizes the unfolding of God's eternal design for human beings.

1. The Groaning of "Creation" (vv. 19-22)

This is one of the most curious and fascinating passages in Romans. Its distinctiveness lies in the fact that here for the first and perhaps only time in his extant letters Paul considers human beings in relationship to the non-human created world. This feature has lent the passage extraordinary interest from the modern reader's point of view. At the same time the text is replete with the kind of mythological and apocalyptic motifs that call for imaginative and suggestive interpretation rather than strict exegesis. All attempts at understanding, however, must proceed from an appreciation of the background of thought from which Paul's argument, if it can be called an "argument," proceeds.

"Common Fate"

Paul presupposes a Jewish tradition which saw the non-human created world as intimately bound up with the fate of human beings. Non-human creation progresses when the human race progresses; it suffers a fall when human beings fall. In short, both share a common fate. The fundamental basis for this is once again the idea expressed in Gen 1:26-27 that human beings, in virtue of bearing God's image and likeness, have a responsibility for "subduing" the earth. More particularly, the motif seems to go back to Gen 3:17-19, where the ground is cursed because of Adam's sin. The result is that instead of its providing for him without effort on his part, now he has to toil and sweat to make it yield its fruits.

So much for the idea of a common "Fall." But also in the Old Testament and based on the same linkage between the human race and the rest of creation, we have the positive converse — the hope for a common restoration. Such an idea lies behind Isaiah's motif of the wolf dwelling with the lamb and so forth (Is 11:6-9) and Second Isaiah's vision of the return to Jerusalem as accompanied by the desert turned into a paradise (41:17-20; 48:9-11; cf. Ezek 34:25-31; 47:1-2).

This "common fate" idea linking human beings and the rest of creation is the hinge upon which Paul's argument in Rom 8:19-22 turns. Creation, fallen with the human race, shares a hope nonetheless that it will share also in its restoration. Sensing that this restoration — or at least its public manifestation — is close at hand, creation becomes restless with its bondage and groans in longing to be free (v. 22). Paul takes this "groaning" of creation as a sure hint that full freedom for human beings is not far off. That is, he takes it as a sign of hope. It is almost as if nature is sensitive to something that human beings do not yet realize — rather like the stationmaster's dog, which can sense the proximity of a train long before the staff or passengers are aware of its approach.

The "Subduer"

Clearly this argument rests upon a highly personified view of creation. But some of the attached theological motifs are worthy of note. In vv. 20-21 Paul is evidently considering the "fall" of creation as told in Genesis 3. Creation when it fell did so "not by its own will but on account of the one who was meant to subdue it." Who is this "subduer"? According to the literal account of Gen 3:17-19 it is God who curses the earth following Adam's fall. However, it makes better sense in the present context and accords with Paul's use of "subdue" elsewhere to follow a longstanding tradition of interpretation and see the "subduer" here to be Adam. As we noted above, the earlier account of creation in Gen 1:26-27 accords to the human race the dignity and task of subduing

the earth, an idea which in terms of Ps 8:6 plays an important role in Paul's view of Christ's messianic reign (1 Cor
15:25-28; cf. Phil 3:21). On this understanding, Paul would
be saying that creation's lapse into "futility" occurred
because Adam, as representative and paradigm of human
beings, abused the God-given task properly to "subdue" the
world. In other words, Paul is again using Adam to tell the
"sin-story" of human history, but this time the emphasis is
not so much upon the unfortunate effects in human nature
itself (as in Rom 1:23; 3:23) as upon the equally disastrous
effects *ad extra,* that is, in the non-human created world for
which humans are responsible.

"Futility"

In this connection it is interesting to note the term Paul
uses to describe creation's fall. He speaks of a lapse into
"futility" (*mataiotêtês*). Through this word the author of
Ecclesiastes summed up his pessimistic view of reality. It
denotes principally the frustration of the purpose of things.
Inanimate creation has been subject "to the frustration of
not being able properly to fulfil the purpose of its existence,
God having appointed that without man it should not be
made perfect" (Cranfield).[1] Beyond this basic sense, how
ever, *mataiotêtês* has connections in Jewish literature with
idolatry. Through the false worship of "the creature in place
of the Creator" (Rom 1:25) not only do human beings lose
their own "glory" or likeness to God but the intrinsic purpose of created things is frustrated.
   This concept of "futility" would not be at all far from the
more modern idea of "alienation." The alienation which
exploitation of resources or of the labor and creativity of
human beings is seen to produce has its foreshadowing in
Paul's view of the disastrous ramifications of human sin. For
Paul a right relationship of human beings to God entails a
constructive relationship to the world. Sin as the selfish

[1] *The Epistle to the Romans* 1.413-14.

exploitation of the God-given human power and dignity destroys the surrounding context as well as humanity itself. It prevents the universe attaining its proper goal.[2]

On the positive side, creation longs for the "revealing of the sons of God" (v. 19) and hopes to be "set free from its bondage to decay to share in the freedom associated with the glory of the children of God" (v. 21). The "revelation of God's sons" stands in parallel with the "glory to be revealed in us" in v. 19. Sonship and glory go together. To be revealed as God's sons means to be publicly revealed as possessing the likeness to God with which is bound up fullness of humanity and, specifically in this context, freedom from death and all diminishment. Believers are already God's children and even now have some share in his glory. But they enjoy this status in a hidden way. Full freedom and public revelation will come with resurrection — as it already has in the case of Christ (cf. Rom 1:4: "designated Son of God in power...from the time of his resurrection from the dead"). It is this full freedom that creation both senses and longs to share.

REFLECTION

As we said above, the uniqueness of this passage lies in the fact that it views the destiny of the human race as wholly bound up with that of the surrounding context, the created world. It assigns to human beings a responsibility for both the past and future of the world and sees that responsibility as an essential element in the relationship to God. As technology and science progress, the human mastery of the world becomes more and more complete, the potentiality for the greatest good and the greatest evil stronger. Ever more clearly we find written in our world traces of both the "grace" story and the "sin" story of human life. Now for the first time technology is so advanced that mastery could paradoxically be played out in total (nuclear) devastation. "Futil-

---

[2]Cf. Kavanaugh, *Following Christ in a Consumer Society* (p. 58, n.3 above) p. 11.

ity" in the Pauline sense could become universal and complete. Likewise for the first time the natural resources for giving all a decent human life are within grasp. The future shape of the world will be a reflection of which "story" — sin or grace — wins out. The basis for hope is the "much more" weighting Paul accords to grace.

2. The Groaning of "Ourselves" (vv. 23-25)

Creation "groans" with respect to what it discerns happening in human beings. Now Paul goes on to indicate a "groaning" of human beings with respect to themselves. "Having the first fruits of salvation in the shape of the Spirit, we groan with respect to ourselves" (v. 23a). "First fruits" is a metaphor from the harvest ritual of Israel. The first fruits of the harvest are taken to the Temple and offered to God both in acknowledgment that the growth has been his gift and as a sign of hope for the full harvest to follow. Thus the gift of the Spirit, the only tangible element of the final state that Christians now possess, is a pledge and guarantee of the complete harvest, full salvation, to follow.

As in vv. 15-16 above, the Spirit functions here as engenderer of hope. It does so by stirring up within Christians a kind of "holy discontent," a "groaning" that is not so much a negative response to pain as a positive restlessness with the present lot, a sense of and a longing for something better to come. This sense of the incompleteness of the present situation is, of course, an element of universal religious experience. Augustine gave it classic expression in his famous sentence about our hearts being restless till they rest in God. Echoes of Paul can be heard in a 17th Century poet's musing on God's holding back the gift of "rest":

> For if I should (said he)
> Bestow this jewell also on my creature,
> He would adore my gifts instead of me,
> And rest in Nature, not the God of Nature.
> So both should losers be.

Yet let him keep the rest,
But keep with them repining restlessnesse:
Let him be rich and wearie, that at least,
If goodnesse leade him not, yet wearinesse
May tosse him to my breast.

(George Herbert, *The Pulley*)

Paul, however, gives some content to this "restlessnesse": it involves awaiting "full sonship, the redemption of our bodies." The word, *huiothesia,* translated here as "full sonship" means "adoption" in ordinary Greek usage. "Adoption" is not, however, particularly appropriate in the present context. If believers are already "sons/children of God," as Paul has clearly stated (v. 16), why should they still be awaiting an act — adoption — initiating that status? Moreover, adoption was not a social custom in use among Jews. For Paul to use it as an image at this point would stand in some contrast with the otherwise thoroughly "Jewish" tenor of his terminology and argument. It is best to see in *huiothesia* a reference to the full possession of the Israelite eschatological privilege of sonship, which as the following phrase suggests reaches its completion at the time of resurrection.

By "redemption of our bodies" Paul does not mean "redemption *from* our bodies" in a Gnostic or even Platonist sense. That would suggest that all becomes well with human beings once they shed attachment to the physical world, an idea at odds not only with Paul's conception of "body" in general but also with what he has just been saying in vv. 19-22 immediately before. By "redemption of our bodies" Paul means the setting free of that aspect of ourselves making for union, solidarity and communication (the sense of *sôma*) from crippling attachment to the passing world and its fallen structures. The phrase looks to the resurrection of the body and the sense of corporate and physical freedom that resurrection will involve.

With this assertion of freedom and resurrection Paul remains content. He has no information to offer concerning the future and chooses to remain in Romans even more "agnostic" in this respect than in the earlier correspondence with the Corinthians (1 Cor 15:35-49; 2 Cor 5:2-5). Instead he offers in vv. 24-25 a little excursus on "hope." "We are in a situation of salvation (the verb tense for once sets salvation in the past), but only in hope." Now if that hope was already clearly in view, if its detailed content was already marked out for us, then our waiting for it would hardly involve the virtue of hope at all. For "who hopes for what he sees?" (v. 24c). The virtue of hope consists in "waiting with endurance" (v. 25b). Paul is both remarkably certain about the fact of God's future and remarkably agnostic about its details.

REFLECTION

Christian hope, then, for Paul does not derive from an optimistic view of the present situation of the world. Nor, in contrast to a Marxist perception, does it spring from the necessary working out of socio-economic forces towards a determined future. It springs entirely from the fidelity of God and from an awareness in faith of his will to bring the world to its proper fulfilment.

Hope rests, then, entirely on God, but not in the sense that his saving action will effect a kind of *deus ex machina* rescue. The whole tenor of the ethical excursus culminating in 8:1-13 has been to suggest that God's fidelity to the world works through human beings — not through works they do on their own account independently of him, but in so far as they "live out" his gift of righteousness, allow his saving justice to "be fulfilled in them" through the Spirit (8:4). In this way the future of the world is both in the hands of God and in the hands of men and women of each age. Hope rests on the "subduer's" cooperation with the "much more" powerful weight of grace over against the power of sin.

3. The Groaning of the Spirit (vv. 26-27)

Paul has just spoken of the "endurance" required when one hopes for what is not seen. As a third witness for hope he now points to the Spirit, who comes to our aid in the weakness that makes this hoping a matter of endurance. The "weakness" Paul means is probably the specific weakness that comes from our "not seeing." We can pray in general terms for salvation, for glory, etc. But because the particular contours of God's future are as yet unknown to us we cannot express our longings in words that have any meaning. In this predicament the Spirit who does know what God has in store for us presents our prayers in appropriate form before God. He is both intercessor and interpreter for us before God.

It has been suggested that the groans uttered by the Spirit refer to ecstatic speaking in tongues in the communities. This interpretation at least has the advantage of making something experiential, albeit unintelligible, the witness to hope. But it is more likely that Paul has in mind an operation of the Spirit that takes place at a depth and a level not normally accessible to human awareness. In 2 Cor 12:3-4 he alludes to an experience of his own when he was rapt up "into Paradise" — whether in the body or out of it, he does not know — and there heard things which "cannot be told, which a human being cannot speak." In this mystical state Paul became aware of "heavenly conversation" not normally accessible to everyday religious experience. It may be that in such privileged moments he gained a glimpse of that continual prayer which he here (Rom 8:26-27) suggests the Spirit carries on continually concerning our future and which he presents as the third "groaning" evidence for hope.

This is an elusive passage. Virtually everything that can be said about it remains speculation. But it may well be a point where Romans touches upon the mystical tradition of Christianity and other religions. Mystical experience, which of course is not so rare as often supposed, involves inward awareness and communication transcending ordinary thought and speech. What can be reported of it does suggest that it bears upon a union with reality or the deity where the barrier between time and eternity slips away, where there seems to be some glimpse and foretaste even of what the perfected union with God might contain.[3] The journey inward is a journey to the future or, to put it in terms more strictly Pauline, is a journey to that hidden glory, hidden reflection of God which the Spirit is nurturing here and now, and of which resurrection will be the revealing. If such considerations are not alien to the present context but in fact bear closely upon what Paul is trying to say, then it is surely interesting that the Paul who placed human beings and their future so firmly in the contest of the surrounding world in vv. 19-22, should find it perfectly natural to move immediately to the more inward, even mystical aspect of religion. For him, clearly, there was no contradiction.

4. The Working out of God's Eternal Plan (vv. 28-30)

Paul has just observed that the prayer of the Spirit is "in accordance with God's will." That is, the Spirit knows the full content of God's plan for the elect and can in consequence pray effectively and appropriately for its completion. The following three verses form a conclusion centered around the unfolding of this plan. The ultimate basis for hope is the fact that God has a plan for human beings, that the various stages of that plan are under way and that what God has begun he will surely, for our benefit, bring to fulfilment.

V. 28 is open to a variety of translations depending on whether the subject of "works for our benefit" is taken to be "all things" or "the Spirit" or "God." The translation opts for the last of these on the grounds that reference to God makes for a better transition to the final series of statements (vv. 29-30), where God is clearly subject. The sentence then asserts the firm belief ("we know") that God will listen to the Spirit's prayer because his whole intent and action is directed to the

---

[3]Cf. F. von Hügel, *The Mystical Element of Religion* (New York: Dutton, 1908) p. 281; E. Underhill, *Practical Mysticism* (New York: Dutton, 1915) 40-44; F.C. Happold, *Mysticism: A Study and an Anthology* (2nd. ed.; Harmondsworth: Penguin, 1970) p. 47.

benefit of those who have been called — the benefit, that is, that they arrive at that destiny which he has designed for them from the beginning.

The entire section then concludes with a step-like series of clauses that spell out the individual divine acts involved in the conferring of this "benefit." The symmetry appears when we set it out as follows:

> Those whom he *chose beforehand*,
> he *preordained*...
> Those whom he *preordained*,
> these he also *called*,
> and those whom he *called*,
> these he also *justified*,
> and those whom he *justified*,
> these he has also *glorified*.

All five verbs in this sequence belong to the language used in the Jewish tradition to describe God's favored acts towards Israel. Paul is now applying this language to the "redefined" Israel, made up of Jews and Gentiles (chap. 4). The favors of "election," "calling," ultimately the eschatological "glorification," are now seen to be focused upon all who respond in faith and so constitute the real Israel.

Only once does Paul interrupt the formal sequence to define more closely the act of God. "Chose beforehand" (lit. "foreknew") stands by itself to indicate the favor of election. But then "preordained" receives further specification: "that they should become sharers in the likeness of his son, so that he might become the firstborn among many brethren." With this key qualification Paul points to the Risen Christ as the exemplar of all God's design for the human race. The language is quite strong. It is not a matter of becoming "like" Christ in a general kind of way. The faithful are to become "sharers," that is, real participants in the way of being (literally "image," *eikôn*) proper to the Risen Lord.

This definition of human destiny in terms of the Risen Christ is elucidated by passages in other letters describing the future of the elect. In Phil 3:20-21 Paul speaks of our awaiting a "Savior, who will transform our lowly body to make it *conformable to his glorious body.*" In 2 Cor 3:18 — a passage we have already noted in connection with the loss of "glory" (Rom 1:23) — Paul speaks of believers "seeing as in a mirror the glory of the Lord" and being transformed by the power of the Spirit "into the same image, from one degree of glory to another." A few sentences further on (4:4) the Risen Christ is explicitly named the "image" of God and conversion is described in terms of "the God who said, 'Let light shine out of darkness' (that is, the Creator God of Genesis 1), making light shine in hearts to light up the knowledge of the glory of God on the face of Christ" (4:6).

These parallels suggest that when Paul speaks in Rom 8:29 of humans sharing in the image of his Son he means their real participation in the glorious way of being that pertains to the Risen Christ as "image" of God. In Christ, as "Last Adam" (1 Cor 15:45) the divine likeness or glory, upon which human dignity and destiny depend, is restored to the human race. The Risen Lord models the fullness of humanity which human beings forfeit when they re-enact the sin history of their first father, Adam. It becomes available to them when they follow in the Spirit his path through obedience to glory. In terms of 1 Cor 15:45, "As we have borne the image of the man of earth (Adam), so we shall bear also the image of the man of heaven (Christ)." Thus God's original plan for human beings will be realized when they share fully the glory of the Risen Christ. At present he is God's "Firstborn Son," alone in his risen glory. When he has other "sons" (of God) publicly sharing that glory, he will be, as the final specification of God's preordination states, "Firstborn amongst many brethren"(v. 29c).

The sequence of divine acts continues in v. 30 through "calling," "justification" and "glorification." "Calling" refers, presumably, to that summoning and gathering of the eschatological Israel that takes place with the preaching of the gospel. "Justification" is, as we have seen the eschatological verdict of acquittal that believers have already heard through God's grace.

The remarkable thing is that Paul also speaks of "glorifi-cation" in the past tense — "these he has also glorified." Although all the other acts in the sequence have already been set in motion, surely "glory" still lies ahead? It may be that Paul uses the past tense here as an expression of cer-tainty — what God has set in motion he will so surely bring to term that we can speak of the final act as done. However, recalling the "revelation" language of vv. 19-21 and also the "process" of glorification described in 2 Cor 3:18, we can admit that there is a sense in which glory, in a hidden way, is already a part of Christian life. Just as Christ's obedience as embodiment of the divine fidelity entailed a (hidden) likeness to God or glory, so when believers are conformed to the pattern of that obedience through the Spirit they are already being transformed into his image from one degree of glory to another. Christians follow the pattern of Christ — but one stage behind, as it were. Their resurrection, like his, will be the full, bodily manifestation of the likeness to God begun in obedience and self-offering (cf. Phil 2:6-11).

REFLECTION

With this vision of human attainment of glory as God's design works itself to completion, the wheel has come full circle. All through Romans so far we have noted how the theme of "glory," though never dominant, appears like a golden thread in almost every passage. It is through "glory" that Paul indicates the destiny of the human race. Its loss "in Adam" is the consequence of sin; its attainment in Christ is the fulfilment of God's plan. Faith restores the relationship to the Creator that makes possible the "catching" of his likeness, his glory. Faith continued in obedience initiates the present, hidden acquisition of glory, one day to be revealed in bodily resurrection. A key feature of Romans 8 is the way in which it sets this "glorification" of human beings firmly within the context of the wider non-human created world. "Glory" is lost and won in relationship to both Creator and creatures. In this way Romans 8 is Genesis 1-2 rewritten

— or, rather, it is Genesis 1-2 coming true, in Christ, for the first and last time.

READING:

H. Balz, *Heilsvertrauen und Welterfahrung* (Munich: Kaiser, 1971) 36-115.

*B.J. Byrne, *'Sons of God' — 'Seed of Abraham'* (Rome: Biblical Institute, 1979) 97-122.

*J.C. Gibbs, *Creation and Redemption* (Leiden: Brill, 1971) 33-47.

J. Jeremias, *The Prayers of Jesus* (London: SCM, 1967) 57-65 (on 8:14-17).

E. Käsemann, "The Cry for Liberty in the Worship of the Church," in *Perspectives on Paul* (Philadelphia: Fortress, 1971; London: SCM) 122-37 (on 8:26-27).

G.W.H. Lampe, "The NT Doctrine of Ktisis," *Scottish Journal of Theology* 17 (1964) 449-62.

*S. Lyonnet, "The Redemption of the Universe," in (R. Ryan, ed.) *Contemporary New Testament Studies* (Collegeville: Liturgical Press, 1965) 423-36.

P. von der Osten-Sacken, *Römer 8 als Beispiel paulinischer Soteriologie* (Göttingen: Vandenhoeck & Ruprecht, 1975) 60-128, 260-87.

*R. Scroggs, *The Last Adam* (Philadelphia: Fortress, 1966; Oxford: Blackwell) 59-112.

12

The Sure Victory of God's Love
8:31-39

Introduction and Theme

³¹What, then, shall we say to all this? If God is for us, who is against us? ³²God, I say, who did not spare his own Son, but gave him up for us all, how could he fail to give us along with him all things?

The Great Assize

³³Who shall make an accusation against God's elect? It is God who justifies. ³⁴Then who shall condemn? It is Christ Jesus, who died for us and (more importantly) rose from the dead, who is at the right hand of God pleading our cause.

Earthly Troubles

³⁵Who shall separate us from the love of Christ? Shall affliction or distress or persecution or hunger or nakedness or danger or the sword? ³⁶As it is written, *For your sake we are being done to death the whole day long. We are reckoned as sheep ready for the slaughter* (Ps 44:22).

Spiritual Foes

³⁷But in all these things we are more than conquerors through him who has loved us. ³⁸For I am persuaded that

neither death nor life, neither angels nor principalities, neither things present nor things to come, neither powers [39]nor height nor depth nor any created thing, will be able to separate us from the love of God that comes to us in Christ Jesus our Lord.

Paul writes a triumphant conclusion to the whole section making up Romans 5-8. As we have already noted, he returns to take up very closely the themes and argument of the opening passage 5:1-11. The writing is highly rhetorical in tone, moving swiftly from one thought to another. But a certain flow of argument can be discerned. Vv. 31-34 center around God's "justification" of Christians at the great eschatological "assize." Vv. 35-39 assert the theme of "non-separation" (from the love of Christ/of God), the threatening forces being first (vv. 35-36) earthly, then (vv. 37-39) spiritual foes.

The defiant opening challenge, "God is for us," virtually sums up the theme of Romans. When there was question of considering the human race in two camps, Jew and Gentile, (2:11; 3:29-30), Paul had insisted on the strict impartiality of God. Now, in a way that catches up the whole idea of "saving fidelity," he is equally insistent that this God is "for" the human race, especially believers, in the face of all hostile threat. Paul argues to this saving "inclination" of God on the same basis as in 5:6-11: the extremity of the love God has already shown (in giving up his Son) grounds the hope that he will most surely bring the process to completion (cf. 5:6, 8-9, 10). The language consciously echoes the description in Gen 22:16 of Abraham's readiness to sacrifice his "own son," Isaac. What God did not in the end require of Abraham he has allowed happen in his own case. This shows the extremity of his love, his being "for us" to the end.

Possessing "All Things"

Paul is confident, then, that God having given up his own Son will most surely "give us all things with him" (v. 32b). In general terms this gift refers to the completion of the chain of divine acts listed in v. 30 — our (public) "glorification." Behind "all things," however, may lie a very rich concept connected with the glory of the elect. In 1 Cor 3:21b-23 Paul admonishes the Corinthians for "boasting in men" and continues:

> For all things are yours: whether Paul or Apollos or Cephas, or the world or life or death or things present or things to come; all belong to you and you belong to Christ and Christ belongs to God.

The list of the "things" which "belong" to Christians according to this text bears a close resemblance to that given in vv. 38-39 of the passage we are studying. Because they "belong" to Christ, who in turn "belongs" to God, Christians share in the triumphant "possession" of the universe exercised by the Risen Lord (cf. 1 Cor 15:24-28 and Phil 2:9-11). Their destiny is to enter into full possession of that "inheritance," of which with Christ they are "co-heirs" (Rom 8:17) and in which the command to "subdue" the universe is properly played out to the glory of God (Phil 2:11).

The eschatological "glorification" is not, then, simply a vague kind of clothing with heavenly glory. It means the realization, in Christ and with him, of that destiny for human beings expressed in Gen 1:26-27 and, more poetically, in Psalm 8. It is in relationship to creation and with it that Christians make full entrance into that inheritance promised to Abraham (4:13) and held out for them through the fidelity of God. That is why "creation," too, "waits with eager longing for the revelation of God's sons" (8:19).

The Great Assize

In a way that catches up the earlier theme of "justification" Paul next (vv. 33-34) evokes the great judgment scene, the final "assize" according to the old apocalyptic program. This can only be a moment of triumph for Christians since the Judge is clearly "for them" in virtue of the justification already pronounced. Moreover, Christ, whose death worked their deliverance from sin, continues in his risen life to foster their cause, standing as powerful advocate before the throne of God.

Who Can Separate?

So Paul puts his final defiant question (vv. 35-39). With such a scenario being realized in heaven, who or what, on earth or in heaven, is going to separate Christians from God's love? Paul first lists the realities of the Christian situation in terms of earthly opposition. It is by no means certain that the Roman community would paint so challenging a picture of everyday Christian life. As the parallel occurring in 2 Cor 4:7-12 suggests, it is more the hardships and perils of the apostolic life which Paul sketches here and illustrates with the quotation from Ps 44:22 (v. 36). In the second list (vv. 38-39) it is the spiritual powers which are defied, that is, those powers which in the apocalyptic worldview threaten the human race and ever seek to bring it, guilty and doomed to destruction, before the final judgment. These are the powers compelled, according to the final stanza of the Christ-hymn in Phil 2:9-11, to acknowledge the lordship of Christ, the ones who walk captive in his triumphant procession according to Col 2:15.

In their present, "between-time" existence Christians feel the attack and onslaught of all these foes. They are even being "given up to death" as Christ was eventually "given up" (v. 32). But in all this they are "more than conquerors" because of God's love (v. 37). The apparent overthrow of Christ by the hostile powers is unmasked by the gospel for what it really was — the victory of God's love and fidelity over those very same powers (cf. 1 Cor 2:8), as shown in the resurrection. So in their conflict with these powers and even in their apparent overthrow by them Christians remain within the firm grasp of God's victorious justice. As Christ was still God's "own Son" and instrument of his purpose even when "given up," so nothing can separate Christians from God's love (v. 39). The suffering of the present time is totally encompassed by God's faithful love and built essentially into the process whereby his saving purpose goes forward.

REFLECTION

Having proclaimed God's fidelity to a sinful world (Romans 1-4), Paul has now (Romans 5-8) shown how Christians as justified sinners are built into the continued working out of that same divine fidelity. Their "justification" places them totally "in Christ" and so builds them into the embodiment of God's fidelity which his obedience represents. This is the foundation of their own obedience. It stamps the pattern of Jesus' life upon theirs — both for suffering and for hope. Their sufferings, even their death (martyrdom) are caught up in God's eternal plan to bring humanity to its true purpose and dignity.

Paul has at this stage analyzed both the "sin" story and the "grace" story of human beings in terms of their relationship to the non-human created world. The relationship to God and the relationship to the world intersect. The two cannot be taken in isolation. With respect to the world, however, Paul's vision leaves something of a dialectic. On the one hand, the world is passing, fallen, the locus of human enslavement. On the other hand, it too has a place, a role in human glory. With respect to human destiny Paul speaks quite confidently, though not in any detail, of "resurrection." How the present world is matched to that remains unclear. The question is perhaps bound up with that lack of clear vision which for Paul is so essential a part of hope. Meanwhile Pauline theology as emerging from Romans 8 would suggest that Christian obedience attempts to place upon the present world the stamp of a world transformed, a world without sin, where the "subduer" is wholly the instrument of grace. The power of destruction (wrath) remains within human hands, the hope of transformation remains the gift of God.

READING:

H. Balz, *Heilsvertrauen und Welterfahrung* (Munich: Kaiser, 1971) 116-23.

*J.C. Beker, *Paul the Apostle* (Philadelphia: Fortress, 1980; London: SCM) 362-67.

N.A. Dahl, "The Atonement — An Adequate Reward for the Akedah? (Rom 8:32)," in (E.E. Ellis and M. Wilcox, edd.) *Neotestamentica et Semitica: Studies in honour of Matthew Black* (Edinburgh: Clark, 1969) 15-29.

P. von der Osten-Sacken, *Römer 8 als Beispiel paulinischer Soteriologie* (Göttingen: Vandenhoeck & Ruprecht, 1975) 23-60, 309-19.

13

God's Abiding
Faithfulness To Israel
9:1-11:36

Chapters 9-11 of Romans make up a treatise on the fate of Israel that could almost stand by itself. But the question of Israel is integral to Paul's gospel and could not have been omitted from his letter to Rome. This is because the mainspring of his argument, as we have noted from the start, has been the righteousness or fidelity of God. God bound himself in fidelity to Israel and entrusted promises of salvation to the "fathers" (Abraham and the other patriarchs). Yet, save for a tiny remnant that has accepted Christ (the Jewish Christians), those promises have not gone through, or at least appear to have been nullified by Israel's unbelief. What confidence, then, can Christians have in the promise and fidelity of God if his original promise has foundered? If with respect to his chosen people there has been so signal a failure, can we be sure that God's saving righteousness and love will really triumph over all obstacles, as the closing lines of chap. 8 so confidently assert? It is not simply a question concerning the Jews. It is a question about God himself and one that presses most deeply upon the Christian Church.

To some extent Paul now takes up and treats more fully the objections first formulated in 3:1-8 and it will be helpful to glance back to that passage before commencing chap. 9. In that early part of Romans it was a question of God's righteousness in the face of Israel's sin and moral failing in general. Now it is a question of his righteousness vis-à-vis the specific failure of the bulk of Israel to recognize Christ.

This is not the easiest nor the most attractive part of Romans. Paul is on tricky ground here, handling issues that are at once intensely personal and deeply theological. Several of his illustrations raise more problems than they solve. He feels his way gradually to the ultimate solution in chap. 11, which goes well beyond, if it does not actually reverse, things he had written about the Jews in earlier letters (cf. 1 Thess 2:14-16; Gal 4:21-30). Moving fairly swiftly, we shall concentrate on Paul's central pursuit: the final triumph of God's fidelity for the benefit of all human beings.

After the introduction (9:1-5), the discussion proceeds in three clearly discernible stages: 1. 9:6-29: (from the aspect of God) the working of God's righteousness has never depended on human response but remains entirely a matter of his own free choice and promise. 2. 9:30-10:21 (from the aspect of human response) the cause of Israel's failure. 3. 11:1-32 (from the perspective of God's mysterious purpose) the ultimate salvation of Israel.

A. The Problem and the Privileges of Israel
9:1-5

Paul's Avowal

[1] I speak the truth in Christ. My own conscience, enlightened by the Holy Spirit, assures me that I do not lie [2] when I say that I have great grief and continual anguish of heart. [3] For I could pray to be myself a curse, cut off from Christ, if it could help my brothers, my fellow countrymen according to natural birth.

Privileges
[4]For they are Israelites, and theirs is the sonship and the glory and the ordinances and the giving of the law and the worship and the promises. [5]and to them belong the fathers and the Christ according to his natural descent. God, who is above all, be blessed for ever. Amen!

Paul gives no formal introduction to the question of Israel, but simply states his anguish. As if to sharpen the intensity still further, he catalogues the Jewish privileges in what appears to be a formal, traditional list (vv. 4-5). Several of the items are familiar to us from the preceding chapters — "election," "calling," "sonship," "glory," "promise." Indeed, what raises the "Israel" question with such intensity is doubtless the fact that he has just tied such privileges firmly and exclusively to the community of believers made up of Gentiles and a small Jewish remnant.

The culminating privilege of Israel is that "to them belongs... the Christ according to his natural descent."[1] But here lies the supreme irony coloring this whole section. It is precisely with respect to this privilege that Israel has failed. She has not recognized the Christ who came from her according to his natural descent, the Christ who embodies the fidelity of God in her regard — whereas the Gentiles have recognized him and come thereby into the destiny originally cast for Israel alone. What, then, has become of God's promise to Israel? Has it, simply, failed? Paul has powerfully set the question.

B. *The Elective Pattern of God's Promise*
9:6-29

Theme
[6a]But it is not as if the word of God has fallen through.

---

[1]Along with most modern commentators, I take the final reference to "God" not as a qualification of "Christ" (indicating his divine status), but as an independent doxology which concludes the list of privileges. For a fair discussion of the question see Robinson, *Wrestling with Romans* 111-12.

Children of the Promise
⁶ᵇFor not all who are descended from Israel are truly Israel
⁷nor are all descendants of Abraham really children (of
God). But the principle runs: [*Only*] *those in the line of
Isaac shall be called your descendants* (Gen 21:1). ⁸This
means that it is not the children of the flesh who are children of God, but it is the children who come through the
promise who are reckoned as his descendants. ⁹For this is
how the word of the promise runs, *At this fixed time I shall
come and Sarah will have a son* (Gen. 18:10).

Jacob
¹⁰And the same principle operated not only in this case, but
also in the case of Rebecca, when she was with child by one
man, our father Jacob. ¹¹While they were as yet unborn
and had therefore had no chance to do anything, good or
bad, in order that God's elective purpose might prevail
¹²and rest not on human deeds but solely on God's call, she
was told, *Let the elder be servant to the younger* (Gen
25:23). ¹³This was in accordance with what Scripture says:
Jacob I have chosen to love, but Esau I have chosen to hate
(Mal 1:2-3).

Objection 1
¹⁴What, then, shall we say? Is God unfair? By no means!
¹⁵For to Moses he says, *I will show mercy to whomsoever I
choose to show mercy and I will have pity upon whomsoever I choose to have pity* (Exod 33:19). ¹⁶So that it all
depends, not on the will of human beings nor upon their
striving for a goal, but upon God's having mercy. ¹⁷For
Scripture says to Pharaoh, *For this very purpose I have
raised you up, that I might display through you my power
and so that my name might be proclaimed throughout the
earth* (Exod 9:16). ¹⁸So then God has mercy on whom
soever he will, but also hardens whomesoever he wills.

Objection 2
¹⁹You will say to me then, "Why, then, does God still find
fault? For who can resist his will?" ²⁰But who are you, sir,
to answer back to God? Can something that has been made

say to its maker, "Why did you make me like this?" [21] Does
not the potter have the right to make from the same lump
of clay one vessel for noble and another for common use?

Application
[22] If, then, God, wishing to display his wrath and to make
known his strength, bore with great patience vessels of
wrath that are ripe for destruction [23] and, on the other
hand, has willed to make known the richness of his glory
upon vessels of mercy, which he prepared beforehand for
glory, is not that his right?

The People of God
[24] These latter vessels are we (Christians), whom he has
called not only from amongst the Jews but also from the
Gentiles.

Hosea
[25] This was just as he says in Hosea, *I will call "my people"*
those who are "not my people" and "my beloved" those
who are "not beloved" (Hos 2:23) [26] *and it shall be that in*
the place where it was said to them, "You are not my
people," there they shall be called "sons of the living God"
(Hos 1:10).

Isaiah
[27] And Isaiah cries out concerning Israel, *"Though the*
number of the sons of Israel be as the sand of the sea, only
a remnant will be saved, [28] for fulfilling and curtailing shall
the Lord make a reckoning on the earth" (10:22; cf. Hos
1:10). [29] And as Isaiah had said earlier on, *"If the Lord of*
hosts had not left some offspring for us, we should have
been like Sodom and become like Gomorrah" (1:9).

As we have seen when dealing with chap. 4, the whole
destiny of Israel is tied to God's promise to Abraham "and
to his seed." All the eschatological blessings of salvation
hang upon this promise. The issue Paul now raises concerns
just who constitutes this "seed of Abraham," the focus of the
promise. If all physical descendants of Abraham, simply by
dint of natural ("fleshly") descent, are "seed" in this sense,

then the promise would have to apply equally to Ishmael and the nation he fathered, the Arabs. But Scripture makes it quite clear that the promise is only to run in the line of Isaac, who in the circumstances of his birth is clearly marked out as a child of the promise (v. 9). Thus we have a first indication that God's promise follows an "elective" pattern. That is, that it is not tied simply to physical descent or race but from the start depends upon his free choice.

Paul pursues this issue into the next patriarchal genera- tion. The promise did not run equally in Isaac's twin sons, Esau and Jacob. On the contrary, before they were even born and therefore before either had the chance to earn or forfeit the grace in any way, God once again showed a clear preference for the younger (Jacob) over the elder (Esau) (vv. 11-13). Not only does this show once again the elective pattern of God's promise. It goes beyond the former case to show that such a pattern proceeds completely independently of any response or reaction on the human side.

These examples, taken from the very beginning of the promise's operation, establish for Paul the pattern it is to follow all through. It is not tied to human descent. It cannot therefore be claimed exclusively by one nation over against all others. Nor in the long run does its operation depend upon human response — on keeping or not keeping of the law, for example. It rests solely upon the freedom and choice of God. Nothing on the human side, not even the apparent failure of Israel, can necessarily be said to have brought about its frustration.

Is God Unfair?

Paul may have shown that the promise operates entirely by God's free choice. But this raises grave problems in its turn (vv. 14-18). First of all, it implies that God is unfair, since his treatment of persons is so unequal. Paul rebuts this suggestion, introducing the attribute of mercy as the quality of God's action towards human beings. Mercy, of its very nature, cannot be claimed or earned. At the same time no human being can stand except by God's mercy alone (cf.

Romans 1-3). Thus we cannot fault God's claim before Moses (Exod 33:19, quoted v. 15) of his right to exercise mercy with sovereign freedom. On the other hand and from the negative aspect, God's dealings with Pharaoh (Exod 9:16, quoted v. 17) show how he can bring about resistance to grace ("hardening") to further his wider designs. In seeking to hold Israel back, Pharaoh becomes willy-nilly an instrument for the display of God's power and the proclamation of his name throughout the world.

Paul may already be paving the way here for his later claim that Israel's current "hardening" serves a wider proclamation of the gospel (cf. chap. 11). But his main point is to insist that God, precisely to be God, must retain his freedom. The promise cannot be captured and its operation held in check by human response or human deserts, good or bad.

This in turn brings back the old objection (cf. 3:7) that if God uses human moral failure (e.g., Pharaoh's "hardening" of heart) to further his purposes, then it is unjust of him to blame human beings for their faults. The objector is worried about human freedom. Paul at least allows the objection to be heard. But his major concern is to safeguard the freedom of God. Echoing Is 29:16, he brusquely reminds (v. 20) the objector that a creature has no right to demand of the Creator an explanation for being made this way and not that. The potter likewise (v. 21) cannot be questioned if he makes from the one lump of clay two vessels, one for noble, the other for ignoble purposes (v. 22). So God, as God, must be free to deal with human beings as he thinks fit.

"Vessels of Wrath" and "Vessels of Mercy"

Having established God's right to shape different groups in different ways, Paul is now (v. 22) ready to examine the verification of this principle in the contemporary situation. The irony is that it is (unbelieving) Israel that plays the role of Pharaoh, whereas the Christian Church, made up so largely of Gentiles, has become the beneficiary of the mercy God promised to Israel through Moses. All this has come about as an expression of God's intent. He has let Israel become in its unbelief "vessels of wrath ripe for destruction" (Paul does not say," "consigned to destruction"). He has endured this situation to "make known his wrath," that is, to show what happens to human beings when they fall out of living relationship with him. On the positive side, to show the richness of his glory, he has brought into being "vessels of mercy." These he had long beforehand in his eternal design destined for "glory." That is, as already stated in 8:28-30, he had determined that they should arrive at that fullness of humanity involved in sharing with the Risen Christ the divine likeness.

These "vessels of mercy" make up, according to v. 24, the Christian Church called into being out of Gentiles and a small Jewish remnant. That such was to be the constitution of God's eschatological people Paul finds verified in Scripture. Hosea (2:23; 1:10) foretold the calling of a "not my people" (that is, the Gentiles) to be God's people, and Isaiah (10:22; 1:9) foresaw the "whittling down" of Israel's number to a small faithful remnant. Paul quotes (vv. 25-29) the relevant texts to prove that the formation of the eschatological community along these (for Judaism totally unexpected) lines really represented the will of God all along.

It is not clear whether Paul already had in mind in this passage the ultimately positive view of Israel's hardening expressed in chap. 11., that is, that it is all part of the divine plan to provide a space for the Gentiles to embrace the gospel. Certainty on this point is lost in the obscurity of vv. 22-23. But Israel, like Pharaoh in v. 17 does serve to exhibit God's power, as well as his wrath. Power is shown in his ability to turn a situation of apparent disaster into one that furthers his plans. That is clear in the case of Pharaoh. It is not unlikely that Paul is already envisaging a culminating display of God's power in that he rescues "vessels of wrath" from the very brink of the destruction for which they are "ripe."

The Freedom of God

Taken in isolation, this passage has given rise to what is possibly the most terrifying theological doctrine ever to emerge from scripture: that of "double predestination." This theory holds that God has from all eternity elected some for salvation and some for damnation, a fate which will run through quite independently of all human response. But in the first case it must be emphasized that Paul does not have the fate of individuals in view, but is taking a collective view of Jewish and Gentile response to God. Moreover, what he says here is only one element of a total theological solution he is working towards in his attempt to square the apparent failure of Israel with the biblical doctrine of election and the fidelity of God. He is above all concerned to defend the freedom of God, to insist that the current situation must be considered both in the light of that freedom and as a consequence of its exercise. This is all but one stone in a whole theological edifice being constructed in these chapters. To isolate it and treat it as a complete theology is totally — and disastrously — misleading. Now we are to follow Paul looking at the question of Israel's failure from the opposite pole — that of human response. What caused the bulk of Israel to fail so signally at what should have been the *kairos* of her history?

C. Israel's Failure to Respond to the Gospel
9:30 - 10:21

The Situation
(9:30) What then shall we say? We have to say this: that the Gentiles, who did not pursue righteousness, have in fact attained it — a righteousness that comes from faith; [31]whereas Israel, pursuing a law that seemed to promise righteousness, did not arrive at what the law required.

The Cause
[32]Why? Because they did not proceed from faith, but as if they could achieve their goal through works. They

stumbled at the stone of stumbling, [33]mentioned in Scripture: *Behold I lay in Sion a stone of stumbling and a rock of offense. But the person who has faith in it will not be put to shame* (Is 28:16).

Expostulation
(10:1) Brothers, the desire of my heart and my constant prayer before God is for their salvation.

Cause, cont.
[2]For I am ready to testify that they do indeed have zeal for God, but a zeal that is not according to knowledge. [3]For not recognizing the righteousness of God and seeking to establish their own, they have not submitted to God's righteousness. [4]For Christ is the end of the law to bring salvation to every believer.

Law-Righteousness
[5]For Moses writes concerning the righteousness based on the law that it is the person who practices all its prescriptions who will have life through it (Lev 18:5).

Faith-Righteousness
[6]But the righteousness that is based on faith speaks as follows: *Do not say in your heart, "Who will go up to heaven?"* (that is, to bring Christ down) [7]or, *"Who will go down into the abyss?"* (that is, to bring Christ up from the dead). [8]But what does it say? It says: *The word is near to you, it is in your mouth and in your heart* (Deut 9:4; 30:12-14) (that is, the word of faith which we preach). [9]Because if *with your mouth* you confess that Jesus is Lord and *in your heart* you believe that God raised him from the dead, you will find salvation. [10]For in the heart is the believing that leads to righteousness and in the mouth is the confession that leads to salvation.

Available to all
[11]For what does Scripture say? *Everyone who believes in him will not be put to shame* (Is 28:16). [12]For there is no distinction between Jew and Greek, but the same Lord of all bestowing his riches upon all who call upon him. [13]For

(as Scripture says) *Everyone who calls upon the name of the Lord shall be saved* (Joel 2:32).

Israel without Excuse
[14]But how are they to call upon one in whom they have not believed? And how are they to believe in one of whom they have not heard? And how are they to hear in the absence of a preacher? [15]And how are preachers to make proclamation if they have not been sent? Yes, but Scripture says, *How beautiful are the feet of those who proclaim good news* (Is 52:7). [16]But not all have heeded the gospel. For Isaiah says, *Lord, who has believed our message?* (53:1). [17]So faith comes from hearing and hearing from the word of Christ. [18]But I say, can it be that they have not heard it? Of course not, (for as Scripture says) *Their voice has gone out to all the earth and their words to the ends of the world* (Ps 19:4). [19]But I say again, perhaps Israel did not understand? But first Moses says, *I will make you jealous of those who are not a nation and stir you to anger with a nation that has no knowledge* (Deut 32:21). [20]Then Isaiah dares to say, *I have been found by those who did not seek me, I have revealed myself to those who did not look for me* (65:1). [21]But of Israel he says, *All day long I held out my hands to a disobedient and contrary people* (65:2).

On the human side the situation is indeed paradoxical. The Gentiles, who did not seek right standing with God, have obtained it through their faith; the Jews who sought it might and main, have failed to obtain it at all. They have failed and they still fail because they go about it the wrong way — seeking to perform the works of the law. To be more precise, they go about it in the "works" way which God's act in Christ has shown to be a hopeless dead-end as far as justification is concerned.

For God sought to strip bare all human illusion, to dethrone self-satisfied expectation of salvation on the basis of presumed privilege and works. As long as such delusion exists, there can be no real relationship between Creator and creature — nor can there be hope of gaining the true humanity flowing solely from that relationship. So God set up a Messiah who was to be a "stone of stumbling" (Is 28:16), quoted v. 33). He reversed all purely worldly standards by offering eschatological justification and salvation through the Crucified.

Though challenging the whole human race, the Cross constitutes for Israel in particular a "scandal," a blockage in her path. Why should God's holy and faithful people need and be given *this* kind of Savior? What becomes of Israel's unique status, her accumulated treasure of faithful works? The Cross demands the relinquishment of all this, a surrender, like that of Abraham, to a God of pure grace who "justifies the ungodly." The sole way around — rather through — this "scandal" is to tread this path of faith. Only in the vision of faith can one perceive the gospel of the crucified Messiah to be not folly and loss but the "power and wisdom of God" (1 Cor 1:23-24). The person who has faith in it will not find it a shameful thing (v. 33b).

God's Righteousness

Paul voices (10:1) once more his personal concern for Israel. He understands the dilemma; he has worked through it himself (cf. Phil 3:4-11). He acknowledges the zeal that Israel has for God, but finds it to be a "zeal not according to knowledge" (v. 2). It is "not according to knowledge" because it fails to recognize what God has done in Christ and clings instead to its own perception of both the task and the achievement. In the words of v. 3, Israel seeks to "establish its own righteousness," neither acknowledging nor submitting to the "righteousness of God."

This language in v. 3 shows that the concept of God's righteousness remains the guiding thread in Romans. As in the original Old Testament concept of *sedaqah,* all righteousness flows from God. There is no human righteousness save as a participation in the righteousness of God, upon which the whole religious and social structure rests. Israel's fault is her failure to participate through faith in the righteousness flowing from God's act of atonement in Christ (3:21-26). She clings to the law, resting her hope of what she believes to be her fidelity to God in terms of the righteousness it demands. But the message of the Cross, shone upon Israel's situation in Romans 2, reveals that hope to be false. Israel has not been faithful, the law encloses her in sin. The further message of the Cross, spelled out in Rom 3:21-26, is that this unfaithfulness does not ultimately matter because God remains faithful to her despite all. In the sacrificial death of Jesus he has provided a means to give even unfaithful Israel reconciliation with himself and also to immeasurably enlarge and extend the scope of salvation.

The law, then, as a means of salvation, is finished. Christ is its "end" (v. 4). To cling to it any longer is to stand up against God's saving righteousness and specifically against his purpose to bestow salvation on the basis of faith to all believers. This resistance on the part of Israel to the full scope of God's righteousness is for Paul the heart of her failure.

So Paul has indicated the fundamental cause of Israel's failure. In the remainder of chap. 10 (vv. 5-21) we are shown why responsibility for that failure rests entirely with Israel and not with God.

The "Nearness" of Salvation

As a first stage of this (vv. 5-13) Paul sets up in rather quaint terms a contrast between the difficulty of the quest for righteousness through the law and the ease or "nearness" of finding it — and ultimately salvation — through faith. He first quotes (v. 5) the words of Lev 18:5 to show how law-righteousness requires an arduous and complete fulfilment if life is to be won. He then (vv. 6-8) takes a text from Deuteronomy (30:12-14), which in its original context proclaims that the "commandment" (of Moses) is neither "hard" nor "far off." In a most arbitrary way Paul strips this text of all reference to performance of the law and makes it speak instead of the ease and "nearness" of finding righteousness by faith. You do not have to drag the (exalted) Christ back from heaven, you do not have to search him out among the dead; you have access to him and to the justification he brings in the preached word of faith. In the words of an earlier text of Deuteronomy (9:4) it is simply a matter of confessing with one's lips and believing in the heart what God has done in Christ. Surrender in faith and trust to the act of divine righteousness that raised Jesus from the dead brings right relationship with God and points one towards salvation (vv. 9-10).

That is what has made salvation available to all (vv. 10-13), what has brought the riches of salvation to the Gentiles, who did not have the law. For the Jews, particularly, it was close at hand. Paradoxically, however, its very simplicity and nearness is what has made the gospel so bitter a pill for them. Because it struck so poignantly at their imagined privilege and status they greeted it, for the most part, with rejection and disbelief.

Israel Without Excuse

In the concluding part of the chapter (vv. 14-21) Paul reviews all the "excuses" which could be mounted on behalf of Israel and dismisses them one by one. He does so largely through Scriptural quotations which even by the canons of his own time are arbitrary and forced. No one who is not already converted, least of all Jews, will be convinced by Paul's use of Scripture here and in the preceding passage. But he is in fact arguing "from inside." He is attempting to show believers that if one reads Scripture in the light of what God has actually done, that is, in the light of Christ, then you can "hear" it speaking the language of righteousness by faith, hear it telling that the present situation of Gentile faith and Jewish unbelief was something foreseen and even planned by God all along.

Israel has had a chance to hear the Scriptures in this new way. Evangelists have gone out and preached throughout the world the gospel that kindles faith. Through their message the voice of Christ (v. 17) still addresses his people. If Israel has not responded, it is not through want of a preacher (vv. 19-21). It is because she has deliberately chosen not to believe.

A Parable

Paul seems to consider unbelieving Israel as being somewhat in the position of a servant entrusted by his master to carry out a mission of great privilege and trust. The servant has received the task with pride and joy, investing much of his personal identity in the charge and jealously guarding the detailed instructions given concerning its execution. Over the years he comes to see his relationship with the master almost entirely in terms of the successful performance of this task. But he does not keep an ear open for what might be any alterations in the master's wishes. Or perhaps from the very start he failed to grasp the deepest meaning of the charge. At any rate he banks entirely on what he sees to be faithful performance, anticipating praise and reward when finally called to account.

When the summons at last comes, the servant is shocked and shattered to find that he has got it all wrong, that he has failed to carry out what the master really wanted. So deep is his humiliation, so crushing the blow to his identity, that he cannot really hear this news. Above all, he cannot hear the master saying that in the end it does not matter, since the relationship in his eyes does not ultimately stand or fall with the performance of the task. A renewed relationship, the one the master intended all along, is being offered to him, one not based on task but on pure acceptance. It is, admittedly, a relationship which he must share with other servants, who have likewise failed and whose failures and less-privileged status he previously despised. But nonetheless his privilege remains if only he could see it. For he treasures the original instructions (the Scriptures) and has the chance to hear them anew and, in the light of the new relationship, discover their real meaning.

CONCLUSION

So, at the close of chap. 10 Paul has considered the situation of Israel and the Gentiles with respect to the gospel from both the divine and the human angle. The "failure" of Israel was in some sense willed by God (chap. 9) and yet it remains the fault of Israel. Paul realized the tension this double truth creates for human freedom (9:19-21). Yet he will not surrender either aspect in the interests of a totally integrated theology. He has run into the age-old problem of harmonizing the omnipotence and plan of God with the full exercise of human freedom. He does not offer a complete solution and to require one of him would be unreasonable. He has simply attempted to show from both the divine and human angle that the failure of Israel to respond to Christ cannot be charged against the faithfulness of God to his promise.

D. The Final Working-out of God's Righteousness: Israel's Salvation 11:1-32

Thematic Question
(11:1a) I ask then, has God rejected his people? Of course not!

1. The Remnant
[1b]For one thing, I myself am an Israelite, of the seed of Abraham, of the tribe of Benjamin. [2]No, God has not rejected his people, whom he chose. Do you not know what Scripture says of Elijah, how he entreats before God against Israel? [3]*Lord, they have killed your prophets, they have overthrown your altars, and I alone am left, and they seek my life* (1 Kgs 19:10, 14). [4]But what does the oracle say to him in response? *I have left for myself seven thousand men who have not bent the knee to Baal* (v. 18). [5]So also at the present time a remnant has come into being, chosen by grace. [6]If it exists by grace, then in no sense does it proceed

any longer from works, or else grace would cease to be grace. [7]What then? What Israel was seeking, this it did not find, but the remnant did find it. As for the rest, they were hardened. [8]As Scripture says, *God gave them a spirit of stupor, eyes that should not see and ears that should not hear, right down to this very day* (Deut 29:4). [9]And David says, *Let their table become a snare and a trap, and a stumbling-block and a source of retribution for them,* [10]*let their eyes be darkened to prevent them from seeing and bow down their back for ever* (Ps 69:22-23)

2. Israel's Fall serves the Gentiles' Salvation
[11a]I ask then, have they stumbled in a such a way that their fall is final? Not at all! [11b]But through their fall salvation has come to the Gentiles, and this to make Israel jealous. [12]Now if their fall has meant the enrichment of the world and the cutting down of their numbers the enrichment of the Gentiles, how much greater will be the effect of their full inclusion. [13]I am speaking here to you Gentiles. Inasmuch then as I am apostle to the Gentiles, I make as much of that ministry as possible [14]so as to provoke my own flesh and blood to jealousy and so save at least some of them. [15]For if their rejection means the reconciliation of the world, what else will their acceptance mean but resurrection from the dead? [16]If the first-fruits are holy, then so too must be the whole lump. And if the root is holy, so also the branches.

[*The Olive*]
[17]Now if some of the branches were cut off and you, a wild olive, have been grafted in among them so as to have a share in the richness of the (cultivated) olive's root, [18]do not vaunt yourselves over the branches. For if you boast you fail to realize that it is not you that is supporting the root, but the root supporting you. [19]You may well say, Branches were cut off that I might be grafted in. [20]Quite so. They were cut off because of their lack of faith. But you stand only through faith. Do not have proud thoughts, but rather stand in awe. [21]For if God has not spared the natural

branches, neither will he spare you. [22]See at once both the kindness and the severity of God: his severity with respect to those who have fallen, kindness towards you — that is, if you continue to remain in his kindness. Otherwise, you too will be cut away. [23]Whereas they, if they do not remain in their unbelief, will be grafted in again. For God has the power to graft them in again. [24]For if you have been cut from what is by nature a wild olive and grafted contrary to nature onto the cultivated olive, how much more easily will these natural branches be grafted back onto their own olive stock.

3. The "Mystery" of Israel's Return

[25]That you may not be wise in your own conceits, brothers, I want you to know about this mystery: a hardening has come upon part of Israel until the full number of the Gentiles has come in. [26]Only by passing through this experience shall all Israel find salvation, as Scripture says: *A Deliverer will come from Sion; he will remove from Jacob all his impieties,* [27]*and this will be my covenant with them, when I remove their sins* (Is 59:20-21; 27:9). [28]As regards the spreading of the gospel they are, for your sake, "enemies"; but as regards God's choice they are, for the sake of the fathers, still "beloved." [29]God's favors and his calling are irrevocable. [30]Just as you were once disobedient to God, but have now received mercy as a result of their disobedience, [31]so now they too have been disobedient for the sake of the mercy granted to you, in order that they also may receive mercy. [32]For God consigned all to disobedience in order that all might experience his mercy.

Hymn of Praise

[33]O the depth of God's wealth, wisdom and knowledge! How unsearchable are his judgments and how untraceable his ways! [34]*For who has known the mind of God? Or who has been his counsellor?* (Is 40:13). [35]*Who has ever given anything to him to receive something in return?* (Job 41:11). [36]For from him and through him and unto him are all things. To him be glory for ever. Amen.

But the last word has not been said. God, in ultimate fidelity to his creatures, can draw human failure into his overall purpose. The unbelief of Israel can serve the cause of universal salvation. It is this hope that Paul sketches in chap. 11. He begins by bluntly facing what seems to be the necessary conclusion from all that has been said: has God (finally) rejected his people? (v. 1) This is roundly denied in the usual fashion. Then follows in three stages the deployment of his positive thesis concerning Israel's future.

First of all (vv. 1-10), he points out that not all Jews have in fact at the present time been rejected. He himself, "an Israelite, of the seed of Abraham, of the tribe of Benjamin" (v. 1b), is a living refutation of this. So too is the Jewish-Christian community within the present Christian Church. This is no mere relic absorbed with loss of identity into the greater number. It represents a faithful "remnant," chosen by God's grace and foreshadowed in his response to Elijah (cf. vv. 2-6). This remnant has achieved what Israel was seeking, but done so wholly on the basis of grace (vv. 6-7c). For the time being it remains the symbol of God's fidelity to Israel.

The rest of Israel has, however, undergone a "hardening" (vv. 7d-10). Paul clearly understands God to be the agent of this "hardening" and in some sense to have willed it (as in the case of Pharaoh, 9:17). Yet it is not clear how the divine hardening relates to the human act of will refusing belief. To some extent the divine purpose antecedes that human rejection, to some extent it locks or clamps human beings into the fatal choice already made. In the latter respect it resembles the "wrath" revealed in the Gentile world according to 1:18-32. When human beings reject relationship with God they wallow helplessly in that rejection, suffering, as Paul sees it, all the ills described in the scriptural quotations in vv. 8-10.

Israel and the Salvation of the Gentiles

But God in his fidelity has not allowed Israel's "hardening" to be either meaningless or final. In the second stage of his discussion (vv. 11-24) Paul advances the daring thesis

that the failure of Israel with respect to the gospel has provided both the scope and the impetus for the enrichment of
the Gentile world by means of the same gospel (vv. 11-12, 15,
23-24). That very enrichment should then serve, according to
Paul's somewhat over-sanguine hope, to stir up the Jews to
jealousy and ultimate conversion (vv. 11, 14). Using the
"much more" kind of argument familiar from chap. 5, Paul
strikes a note of great optimism in respect of this hope: if
the failure of Israel has been the occasion of such enrichment, how much greater will be the consequences of their
return (v. 12): will it not mark the triumphant consummation
of all things in the resurrection of the dead (v. 15)?

The extended image of the "wild olive" grafted on to cultivated stock (vv. 17-24) precisely reverses what would be normal horticultural practice. Paul has been criticized for
employing an image which he as a townsman got hopelessly
wrong. But the "unnaturalness" of the procedure is precisely
the point he wants to make. The Gentiles, the "wild olive"
grafted in, are warned not to repeat the sin of the Jews in
despising the (unbelieving) branches now cut off. These
remain "holy" because the "root" (that is, the Jewish-
Christian remnant) is holy (v. 16). And God who performed
the more "unnatural" feat of grafting the wild olive can (and
will) all the more easily graft in again the natural stock. The
implication is clear: unbelieving, Israel, though "hardened,"
remains both "holy" and the object of God's saving intent.

The Mystery of Israel's Return

In his third and final stage (vv. 25-32) Paul proclaims the
return of "all Israel." This is a "mystery," that is, an element
of God's eschatological plan, hidden from ordinary human
view and contrary to the apparent run of history, but
revealed through prophecy to the elect. The "mystery" here
concerns the foreseeing not so much of Israel's return as of
her return in the way described — that is, via the "hardening" and after the return of the Gentiles. This view precisely
reverses the standard Jewish apocalyptic expectation where

the Gentiles stream to an already glorified Sion.

In the concluding verses (vv. 28-32) Paul spells out first the basis, then the reason for the operation of the mystery in this way. The basis of the hope for Israel's return is that God's "favors" and his "calling" are irrevocable. Here we see the fundamental principle of Romans — God's abiding fidelity — carrying Paul's thesis home to its conclusion. Human failure cannot be allowed to have the last word over against God. If Israel was the first beneficiary of God's favor, Israel will be included in the end.

The purpose of this mode of operation is that Israel, along with the rest of the world, might experience the mercy of God. The Creator wishes to deal with all not as a God who rewards human effort, nor as one who punishes irrevocably, but as one whose fidelity manifests itself as mercy. Thus the general "disobedience" (Gentile and Jewish), at one level the culpable failing of human beings, is in some way also the design of God. He has "consigned" all (Paul has in mind Jews and Gentiles collectively rather than individual human beings) to disobedience, so that all might experience mercy — that is, experience him primarily as a God who works salvation through mercy.

Paul's positive hope for Israel rests, then, on his conviction that God's saving fidelity will ultimately triumph. It is a triumph that must completely reverse human expectation and fly in the face of present evidence. In his confidence that it will nonetheless go through, there remains for Paul nothing else but to bring his tracing of the divine fidelity (Romans 9-11) to a conclusion by hymning the inscrutable richness and wisdom of God (vv. 33-36).

REFLECTION

Paul's handling of the fate of Israel in Romans 9-11 has set him wrestling with the age-old problem of reconciling human freedom (and hence the possibility of human non-cooperation) with the prior disposition and on-going will of God. He is compelled to view "the facts" — the fall of Israel

— as both freely-willed human failure and at the same time as somehow part of the divine purpose. He cannot totally reconcile the two, nor can he let either aspect go. For Paul, as for the Jewish tradition generally, God does not stand above human events, observing and judging. God is intimately involved — involved even in the failure and the tragedy; that is the meaning of the "wrath." At the same time precisely because God is involved, the pattern of events is never something lying totally at human disposition. Behind them, pursuing them, leading them, shaping them towards a goal, lies the divine fidelity and therein rests hope.

Whatever be judged the success of Paul's theologizing about Israel's destiny, his view that the Jewish community as yet unbelieving in Christ retains both its "holiness" and its significance precisely as a community, is one that Christians cannot neglect. In Christian history the warnings voiced by Paul to the "wild olive" have largely gone unheeded and his ultimately optimistic view of Judaism has not on the whole prevailed. Tragically, only the appalling excesses of the Holocaust have caused Christian communities to officially endorse the mature Pauline view expressed in Romans 9-11.

More generally, though, the pattern of divine fidelity set out in these chapters bears upon every human community, all human projects, and indeed every human life. All have their measure of continual failure and lack of response. All are marked by that culpable disobedience which Paul found written in every page of Israelite as well as Gentile history. Some may appear "blocked" and "hardened" therein, seemingly without hope. Yet all are pursued by that same victorious fidelity, all are meant to be grasped and transformed by mercy. In acknowledging this and surrendering to it lies for Paul the path to fullness of life.

READING:

C.K. Barrett, "Rom 9:30 - 10.21: Fall and Responsibility of Israel," in *Essays on Paul* (London: SPCK, 1982; Philadelphia: Westminster) 132-53.

*J.C. Beker, *Paul the Apostle* (Philadelphia: Fortress, 1980; London: SCM), Chap. 15: "The Destiny of Israel," (pp. 328-37).

N.A. Dahl, "The Future of Israel," in *Studies in Paul* (Minneapolis: Augsburg, 1977) 137-58.

E. Dinkler, "The Historical and the Eschatological Israel in Rom. 9-11," *Journal of Religion* 36 (1956) 109-27.

G.E. Howard, "Christ the End of the Law: the Meaning of Rom 10:4ff.," *Journal of Biblical Literature* 88 (1969) 331-37.

*E. Käsemann, "Paul and Israel," in *New Testament Questions of Today* (Philadelphia: Fortress, 1969; London: SCM) 183-87.

J. Munck, *Christ and Israel: An Interpretation of Romans 9-11,* Philadelphia: Fortress, 1967.

D. Zeller, *Juden und Heiden in der Mission des Paulus* (Stuttgart: Verlag Kath. Bibelwerkes, 1973) 109-33, 202-69.

14

The Justice of God
in Everyday Life
12:1-15:13

Chapters 12-15 of Romans relate the great theological concerns of the earlier part of the letter to the everyday life of Christians in community. The issue of the relationship between Jews and Gentiles under the overarching rubric of God's mercy and grace is now distilled into a series of exhortations largely concerned with mutual relationships — of Christians with one another and, to a lesser degree, with the surrounding world.

To what extent the exhortations are general in nature and reflect Paul's widespread experience of the difficulties encountered by Christian communities, to what extent they are shaped by his awareness of and concern for particular situations in the Roman community remains a matter of some dispute. Our knowledge of that community's situation is to a large degree somewhat circumstantial. However, we do know that it was a mixed community made up of Jewish and Gentile components. We know also that the Jewish community as a whole had not long before suffered expulsion from the imperial capital and had been allowed to return on the basis of a very slender tolerance. Virtually the whole content of Romans 12-15 can be related to historical factors such as these. There are good grounds, then, for believing that Paul was well informed on the Roman situation and shaped his exhortation accordingly.

In comparison with the earlier chapters this concluding part of Romans raises less difficulty for the modern reader. I shall leave it to be read in the standard translations and propose to comment upon three areas only: 1. 12:1-2, the introductory verses, which state the theological insight undergirding the whole exhortation; 2. 13:1-7, the exhortation concerning Christian attitude to the State, a passage of some controversy in recent times; 3. 15:7-13, the conclusion to Paul's appeal to the "Strong" and the "Weak" to live in mutual harmony and tolerance — a passage which in a significant way resumes the central theme of the whole letter. The latter part of chap. 15 (vv. 14-33), outlining Paul's personal motives and plans, has already been discussed in the Introduction.

A. Christian Life in the Body: Spiritual Worship
12:1-2

> (12:1) I urge you, therefore, brothers, through the mercies of God, to offer your bodies as a living sacrifice, holy and pleasing to God, your spiritual worship in fact. ²And do not be conformed to the pattern of this age, but be transformed through the renewal of your mind, so as to be able to discern what is the will of God: what is good, acceptable and perfect.

Paul has brought his theological exposition in Romans 1-11 to a close around the concept of God's mercy (11:30-32). He has just swept his readers up into a hymn to God's wisdom and knowledge (vv. 33-36). The exhortatory section, which is largely concerned with mutual relationships in the community, continues these motifs. Paul entreats his readers "through the mercies of God": that is, the mercy which has characterized God's dealings with them must now be reflected in and govern their relationships with one another. Secondly, the outward pattern of their lives must constitute a continuation of that "worship" and praise of God into which they have just been swept.

Paul relates this "worship" explicitly to the body. Christians are to offer their bodies as a "living sacrifice" in "spiritual worship." How the "body" is to feature in a worship that is "spiritual" (*logikê*) becomes clear once we recall that "body" for Paul denotes primarily the whole pattern of relationships and communication by which individuals are in touch with the surrounding world of persons and events. "Spiritual worship" in this sense means letting this whole relational pattern of life be drawn into a living praise of God. All aspects of life, including the "physical," must bear the character of worship and, conversely, worship must touch the whole of life. This does not mean the rejection of cultic activity strictly so-called — liturgy and so forth. But it does exclude any cult that does not somehow impinge upon and gather up life.

Moreover, because Christians are anchored to the old, passing world through their bodies it is precisely in the body that they suffer the onslaught and buffets exacted by that world. Bodily service, then, frequently takes a sacrificial shape, perhaps even unto death. In this sense the offering up of the body constitutes a "living sacrifice," continuing the offering of Christ and constantly drawn into its rhythm of self-giving love through the Eucharistic sharing and proclamation (1 Cor 10:16-17; 11:24-26).

But, while joined to the present world in this bodily way, Christians are also radically removed from its alienation and its fate. Hence they are not to be "conformed" to its pattern (v. 2). In so far as imprisoning attachments are concerned, Christians have to "put to death the deeds of the body" (Rom 8:13). They are to let themselves "be transformed through the renewal of their minds so as to be able to discern what is the will of God." In these words Paul sets up what might be called an "ethic of discernment." Christians are to apply their critical faculty (*nous*), set free from conformity to the values of the old world and patterned upon the "mind" of Christ (Phil 2:5), so as to judge, in each situation (and, we might add, in each age) what is "good, acceptable and perfect." An ethic of conformity to a pre-given, fixed code of law is replaced here by one that calls for discernment and reasoning, in the light of God's eternal design for humanity as revealed in Christ.

B. *The Christian and the State*
13:1-7

(13:1) Let every person be subject to the governing authorities. For there is no authority that does not stem from God and those in power have been set up by him. ²So that the person resisting authority resists the disposition of God and those who resist draw down punishment upon themselves. ³For rulers are not a source of dread to good behavior but only to bad. If you want to be free of fear of the authority, then do what is good and you will in fact receive his approval. ⁴For he is God's minister working for your good. But if you do what is wrong, then be afraid. For he does not bear the sword to no purpose; he is God's minister executing punishment on the wrongdoer. ⁵Therefore it is necessary to be subject — not only through fear of punishment, but also for conscience' sake. ⁶For this same reason also you pay taxes, for the authorities are God's ministers constantly attending to this very thing. ⁷Discharge your obligations to all: whether it is a question of tax or levy or respect or honor; give all these to whomsoever they are due.

This small passage has borne a heavy weight of interpretation down the centuries. Both theorists and practicioners of power have found in it a source of legitimation and security — not always to the advantage of the ruled. In recent years it has understandably shared something of the notoriety attending other statements in Paul manifesting a distinct "social conservatism" (e.g., the role of women, 1 Cor 11:2-16;

14:33b-36; instructions to slaves, 7:21-24; and so forth). A reading of Romans that claims to be addressing Paul's gospel in its fullest scope cannot afford to bypass this controversial passage.

Paul appears here to give unqualified legitimacy to an all-powerful institution of this present, fallen world. He insists on subservience to its officials as representatives of God, not merely out of necessity but even "for conscience' sake" (v. 5). Abuses of political power are not considered. There is no "eschatological reserve," no suggestion that the present world and its institutions are being done away with — no hint that all worldly power and authority has been subjected to Christ. Paul simply assumes a religious legitimation of authority common to both the pagan and Jewish tradition and imposes that argument upon his fellow Christians. To borrow one of his own expressions, "What are we to say to this?"

First of all, the passage cannot be dismissed as a foreign body or interpolation in Romans. It may seem isolated and disruptive at first reading. But closer inspection reveals links to the immediate context (cf., e.g., the concepts of "retribution/punishment," "owing/debt"). In fact, authenticity granted, it is precisely the context that must regulate interpretation. Occurring in the exhortatory part of Romans, the passage cannot yield a formal theology of the state. Paul is not here constructing religious political theory. He is simply employing the standard theory of his time to address a particular situation in Rome warranting his concern. It is highly questionable, exegetically speaking, to erect general theory from his passing exhortation.

The precise situation Paul addresses we do not know for sure. The passage reflects none of the hatred for the Roman state that later persecution wrung out of the author of Revelation. Paul writes at a time when systematic persecution of Christians still lay ahead. Nonetheless, as we have already noted, the situation of the Christian (as also the Jewish) community in Rome was ever precarious. Its very existence could be threatened by elements hostile to or careless of subservience to state officials. Differences of opinion in this matter could well have been a factor in community dispute. Moreover, if the Jewish Christians included a Zealot minority opposed to the payment of tax (cf. vv. 6-7), such divisions could well have run along racial lines, as chaps. 14-15 seem to suggest. It is well understandable that Paul, aware of such tendencies, should issue a word of warning, not hesitating to bolster it by invocation of the divine authority traditionally held to sanction civil power.

Some more detailed observations. First of all, let us note that, despite titles appended in some translations and commentaries, Paul does not demand "obedience" (*hypakoê*) to authorities but "subjection" (*hypotagê*). The subservience required is not, then, simply identical to the obedience rendered "in Christ" to God (chap. 6). Nonetheless, while pointing out along prudential lines the punishment that non-conformity risks (vv. 3-4), Paul requires conformity not merely from necessity but for "conscience' sake." "Conscience" here, as in 2:15, denotes self-awareness and consent. Such an inner attitude must accompany any human act to make it, in Paul's view, truly human. He means, then, that Christians when conforming to state requirements are to do so conscious that in such involvements they encounter the will of God.

But it is an error in interpretation to press out of this passage more than it contains and hold that the state and its institutions always and in whatever form remain entitled to subservience and respect. As we have noted, Paul does not envisage situations where power is abused, rights infringed, legitimacy forfeited. He has in mind the autocratic Roman state, in whose administration Christians at the time played no active role and against which protest or revolt could only end in disaster. His maxims cannot be transferred without qualification to the modern situation where full-scale participation in the democratic process is a reality or at least a reasonable aspiration.

Sometimes through participation Christians can help make the institutions of state genuine anticipations of the coming kingdom. In some situations, like the community Paul addressed in Rome, they may have scope for little more than conformity in the face of *force majeure*. In others a genuine discernment (12:2) might lead to protest and revolt. It is hard to see that Rom 13:1-7 either excludes or commands any one of these options absolutely. The abiding positive import of the passage consists in its insistence that Christians do not constitute an eschatological elite wholly detached from relations with the fallen, passing world. On the contrary, the institutions of that world, flawed and provisional though they be, are places for "bodily worship" (12:1). In the world and nowhere else in the present time is the new humanity, through the Spirit, coming to be.

C. Israel and the Gentiles — One People Glorifying God 15:7-13

In the final part of his exhortation to the Romans, 14:1-15:13, Paul addresses a more specific question: the division between two groups in the community whom he designates "the Strong" and "the Weak" respectively. The point of dispute centred upon food — whether one should refrain from eating meat and drinking wine, either totally or on certain days. Those described as "Weak in faith" practiced such abstention and may have sought to impose it generally. The "Strong," on the other hand, held all such scruples in disdain. In seeking to identify these groups it is natural to see the "Weak" party as made up of former Jews who retained strict food-law observance from their pre-conversion days, while the "Strong" would be Gentiles, in whose religious life such restrictions had never had any place or meaning. This identification along racial lines is probably in the main correct. But to press it rigidly would be wrong. The Jewish-Christian group doubtless numbered some who, like Paul himself, had found their way to a less scrupulous observance.

Paul's view that "the kingdom of God does not consist in food and drink, but in righteousness and peace and joy in the Holy Spirit" (14:17) clearly aligns him with the "Strong." However, he is careful not to impose this attitude. Instead, his whole exhortation here centers around a plea for mutual acceptance. The overall theme is "Accept one another as God has accepted you" (14:1-2; cf. 15:7); in more christological terms, "Seek not your own interest, but that of your fellow Christian, after the pattern of Christ who 'did not please himself' (15:2-3; cf. 14:7-9)."

Rounding off this exhortation, Paul prays that God may grant the entire community to share the same mind, "so that all together with one voice" they "may glorify the God and Father of our Lord Jesus Christ" (15:6). In conclusion he sets this mutual acceptance and united glorification upon a theological basis which resumes the central thesis of the entire letter:

Theme
(15:7) Therefore, accept one another, seeing that Christ has accepted you, for the glory of God.

Basis
[8]For I am saying that, in response to God's fidelity, Christ has performed a minstry among the Jews to implement the promises made to the fathers, [9]and so that the Gentiles should glorify God for his mercy. As it is written: *Therefore I shall praise you amongst the Gentiles and sing psalms to your name* (Ps 18:49), [10]and again it says *Rejoice, O Gentiles, with his people* (Deut 32:43), [11]and again, *Praise the Lord, all you Gentiles and let all the peoples praise him* (Ps 117:1), [12]and again Isaiah says, *There shall come to the Root of Jesse, the one who arises to rule the Gentiles; on him the Gentiles shall set their hope* (11:10).

Blessing
[13]May the God of hope fill you with all joy and peace in your believing, so that you may overflow with hope through the power of the Holy Spirit.

Paul grounds his call for mutual acceptance upon the "acceptance" both parties, Jewish and Gentile, have received from Christ. The Greek of vv. 8 and 9 is notoriously difficult to construe and how precisely the two aspects of Christ's "service," to Jews and Gentiles respectively, are related is not clear. It is highly likely, however, especially in the light of Romans 4, that the "promises to the fathers" relate not only to the future of Israel but have the enrichment of the Gentiles in view as well. In this sense when Christ fulfilled his messianic role among the Jews this was not only an exercise of God's fidelity to Israel but also an implementation of his promise to Abraham that he should be the "father of many nations" (Gentiles — Rom 4:17-18). So the Gentiles can join with God's (first) people in glorifying God (vv. 9-10). His fidelity to his promise to Israel is at one and the same time an exercise of his mercy towards them.

Thus the simple exhortation to put aside differences in the matter of food — or at least to not let those differences affect their basic oneness — flows from a sense of what the entire gospel is about. The community at Rome, made up of Jews and Gentiles, is invited through mutual harmony and tolerance to give expression to God's whole design for the human race proclaimed in the gospel. Their "acceptance" mirrors and extends the "acceptance" God is holding out graciously in Christ, an acceptance inviting all peoples to respond in one act of glorification and to rejoice in one hope.

In this final "systematic" statement in Romans we find that the wheel has come full circle. All began in 1:18-32 with the message of doom and wrath lying upon the Gentile world because of its failure to "glorify" God. Now through his faithful work in Christ God has drawn the Gentile world back to glorification and in this given them "hope" (v. 12). The entire world may glorify God and find, through his fidelity, the way thereby to fullness of humanity and life.

READING:

Romans 12:
C. Evans, "Rom 12:1-2: The True Worship," in (L. de Lorenzi, ed.) *Dimensions de la vie chrétienne (Rom 12-13)* (Rome: Abbaye de S. Paul h.l.m., 1979) 7-33.

H.E. Stoessel, "Note on Rom 12:1-2: The Renewal of the Mind and Internalising the Truth," *Interpretation* 17 (1963) 161-75.

Romans 13:
E. Bammel, "Romans 13," in (E. Bammel and C.F.D. Moule, edd.) *Jesus and the Politics of His Day* (Cambridge: Cambridge University, 1984) 365-83.

*E. Käsemann, "Principles of the Interpretation of Romans 13," in *New Testament Questions of Today* (Philadelphia: Fortress, 1969; London: SCM) 196-216.

C. Morrison, *The Powers that be,* London: SCM, 1960.

Romans 15:
S.K. Williams, "The 'Righteousness of God' in Romans," *Journal of Biblical Literature* 99 (1980) 241-90, esp. 285-89.

D. Zeller, *Juden und Heiden in der Mission des Paulus* (Stuttgart: Verlag Kath. Bibelwerkes, 1973) 218-33.

Conclusion:
Paul's Theological Vision
in Romans

We have attempted to follow closely Paul's exposition of the gospel in Romans. We have considered the background he presupposes, studied his language with some precision and tried to enter imaginatively into his world of thought. With what theological vision do we emerge from this "close reading" of the text? It seems appropriate to offer by way of conclusion some total view of the theology of the letter. At the same time one is conscious that an attempt to cull a synthesis or systematic exposition of theology from Romans may well be something that would leave Paul himself behind and in fact do violence to the contingent and provisional aspect of his thought.

Rather than attempt such a synthesis I propose to formulate a series of "theses" gathered around three heads: 1. "God"; 2. "Christ"; 3. "Human Beings." These theses will include ideas which, to my mind, Paul presupposes as well as those which he explicitly formulates.

In no sense should this set of (40) theses be regarded as a final, definitive statement about Romans. The best thing by far would be for readers to formulate a personal set of theses and use what follows as a check list for purposes of comparison and challenge. In any case the theses are not meant to substitute for the reading of the text and will, possibly, make little sense apart from such a reading.

God

1. The God of Romans is the Creator God, who raises the dead and calls into being things that do not exist. (Romans 1, 4).

2. The God of Romans is also the faithful God who in his abiding fidelity towards Israel is constantly at work to nourish, recreate and restore the good order and well-being of his people.

3. Only in vital and acknowledged relationship with God as Creator can Israel or human beings in general or the entire social fabric survive. The distortion or withering of this relationship with the Creator brings "wrath" and ultimately destruction. (Romans 1-2).

4. God does not remain indifferent to human infidelity, nor does his election or favor shield human beings (Israel) from suffering the consequences ("wrath") of a distorted or ruptured relationship with himself. (Romans 1-2).

5. At the same time, faced with human infidelity, God exercises his righteousness precisely by seeking to break the grip of sin and restore the relationship to full vitality. (Romans 3).

6. In the Old Testament God's gracious and effective renewal of the covenant relationship was signified by the sacrificial cultus, especially through the expiatory effect of the yearly Day of Atonement ritual. Paul understands God's action in Christ as the culminating and final (eschatological) instance of this act of gracious reconciliation. (Romans 3).

7. In the person of "his own Son" God endured the cost involved in offering this reconciliation to (as yet) sinful human beings. (Romans 5, 8).

8. In Christ God performs this gracious exercise of his fidelity not merely for the sake of Israel but for the benefit of the whole world. Catching up the universalist vision of Second Isaiah, foreshadowed in the wide scope of the original prom-

ises to Abraham, Paul sees the God of Israel as the Creator reaching out in fidelity to the entire sinful world. (Genesis 12; Isaiah 42, 49, 60; Romans 1, 3, 15).

9. In this way God has set in motion the plan for human beings evolved from the beginning of creation. Having set this plan so triumphantly in train, he will in continuing fidelity most surely bring it to fulfilment. (Romans 5, 8).

10. God's act in Christ confirms what the Scriptures had already indicated: that he will not have any relationship with human beings save one based on his gracious acceptance of the sinner, responded to in faith. (Romans 3-4, 9, 10).

11. God requires obedience of human beings. But obedience of itself cannot establish a relationship with him. It must *flow from* the relationship already established by God's acceptance (grace) and human response (faith). (Romans 4).

12. God remains faithful to his promises, but their working out always respects his sovereign freedom and grace. (Romans 9).

13. All human understanding of God's purposes and ways, even the most traditional, has to respect this freedom and so be regarded as provisional. All is subject to revision in the light of God's act in Christ. This has become the sole interpretative key to Scripture and all else. (Romans 9).

14. God is able to draw human failure and sinfulness, even the initial rejection of Christ, into the victorious scope of his wider saving purpose. (Romans 7, 11).

Conclusion: The God of Romans, while utterly transcendent as Creator, is not a remote, Olympian deity, but a God who constantly and faithfully strives to renew, restore and bring to full effect the relationship between himself and creation.

Christ

15. From the "side of God," Jesus as "sent" Son of God represents the invasion of God's saving righteousness into

the fallen human world. His total "career" embodies the fidelity of God to Israel, to the entire human race and to creation as a whole. (Romans 3, 8, 15).

16. From the human side, Jesus as "Last Adam" successfully replays the role of Adam as patriarch of the human race. (Romans 5; 1 Corinthians 15).

17. His obedience consists in remaining faithful, in the fullest sense and "unto death," to the demands of a human being living in vital relationship with God. (Romans 5).

18. This obedience, in that it led inevitably to fatal conflict with powers opposed to God, involved faith in a God who in power and fidelity raises the dead. (Romans 5; 2 Corinthians 4).

19. Jesus' acceptance of death in this spirit of obedience and faith follows the pattern of the martyr's death, which is appropriately described as *hilastêrion,* in that through it God effects expiation of sin and (eschatological) renewal of relationship with himself. (Romans 3).

20. The raising of Jesus from the dead represents, in the first place, God's public, bodily "justification" of him as the sole obedient one. It also breaks open the new eschatological relationship with God for all human beings who in faith accept God's gracious offer of association with Jesus. (Romans 4; Philippians 2).

21. As true "image" of God in his bodily risen glory, Jesus is the model and exemplar of that fullness of humanity intended by God as the final destiny of human beings. (Romans 8; 2 Corinthians 4).

22. The Risen Jesus continues to "live to God" in obedience and self-giving love in the lives of those who through faith and baptism live "in" him. Their "spiritual worship" represents the continuance of his own bodily involvement with the world. (Romans 6, 12).

Conclusion: Jesus, then, embodies both the "downward" thrust of God's abiding fidelity to the world *and* the perfect human response to God. While coming "from the side of God" and involving God in the "cost" of redemption, he also plays out totally and successfully the whole pattern of human existence before God. The two "axes" of divine and human fidelity meet in him. Thus we find in Romans a christology "from above" and a christology "from below" meeting without apparent tension. In Paul's view, it would appear, Jesus embodies the divine precisely as totally and fully human.

Human Beings

23. Paul accepts totally the anthropology of Gen 1:26-27, developed in the Jewish tradition, according to which human beings are created in the image and likeness of God. This "likeness to God" is the foundation of human dignity and destiny. Only in living relationship with him as Creator can that dignity and destiny go forward. (Romans 1).

24. According to this same tradition, human beings become like to that which they worship. When they worship or glorify God as God, they acquire his likeness ("glory"). When they give themselves in worship to anything less than God they forfeit their likeness to God and take on the likeness of that which they now worship and become enslaved to it. (Romans 1; 2 Corinthians 3).

25. In view of human freedom, two "stories" can be told of human beings, both historically and actually: 1. an "Adam" story of rebellion and fundamental refusal to acknowledge God as God, issuing in "disobedience" and entraining death; 2. a "Christ" story of response to God in obedience and faith, leading, despite physical death, to the fulfilment of human destiny in eternal life with God. (Romans 5).

26. The historical ratification of the "Adam" story in human lives both proceeds from and enhances a collective bind in sin and destructiveness, which antedates the history of each individual human life. (Romans 5).

27. The historical obedience of Christ has inaugurated a ("much more" powerful) solidarity in grace, right-relationship to God and destiny to life. (Romans 5).

28. Each individual human person lives out his/her life within the tugs of both solidarities and must constantly choose which story is to be ratified in his/her moral life. (Romans 8).

29. Any moral endeavor that attempts to bypass God's work in Christ and does not proceed from the renewal of the relationship graciously offered therein is doomed to founder upon the rock of basic human rebelliousness ("sin in the flesh"). A moral framework imposed from without ("law") cannot successfully address this problem and in fact only serves to exacerbate it. (Romans 7).

30. Obedience is possible because, in sending his Son, God broke the grip of sin upon human beings and thereby released a freedom for obedience, which becomes available to all through the gift of the Spirit. Thus all human obedience remains fundamentally the creation of the triune God, the continuation in the Spirit of God's saving righteousness. (Romans 8).

31. Because life flows from righteousness (that is, from the renewed relationship with God), there is an intrinsic link between human obedience and God's future for the world. God pursues his purpose and exercises his righteousness through the bodily obedience of human beings, which continues in the Spirit the obedience of Christ. (Romans 6, 8).

32. Since the righteousness created in them through the Spirit remains God's righteousness, the future is always both gift and task for human beings. (Romans 8).

33. Hope does not spring from sight of the future, nor from an optimistic assessment of human capacity to fulfil it successfully. Hope rests entirely upon the fidelity of God who in and through human freedom mysteriously pursues his plan for the world. (Romans 8, 9).

34. The human relationship to God encompasses also the human responsibility for the non-human created world. The telling of the "Adam" story in human life redounds disastrously and destructively upon the created world and issues in the frustration of its purpose ("futility"). The realization of the "Christ" story does not reject the world but seeks to transform it into a proper milieu for the living out of the new relationship with God. (Romans 8).

35. In the present "in-between" existence, anchored bodily in the world, human beings remain within the cycle of death and decay. But the pledge of resurrection assigns the last word to God, who through his Spirit is already at work impressing upon this world the relationships and structures of the new. (Romans 8).

36. Thus even in this present existence human beings can arrive in a hidden way at the fullness of humanity and freedom that flows from the eschatological relationship with God ("*Abba,* Father"). (Romans 8).

37. Martyrs most perfectly exhibit this maturity of present human life in that, following the pattern of Christ, they deliver their whole existence up totally to the saving fidelity of God reaching out to humanize the world.

38. But all Christian obedience, since it embodies the fidelity of God towards an only partially reconciled world, retains an element of martyrdom and of continuing faith in a God who raises the dead and calls into being things that do not exist. (Roman 6; 2 Corinthians 4).

39. The Jewish People, despite the historical rejection of Jesus as Messiah, retain their distinctive identity as people of election and remain within the scope of God's saving purpose. (Romans 11).

40. In the preaching of the gospel the once-for-all eschatological exercise of God's righteousness in Christ is made available to all subsequent generations, so that they may receive the fullness of humanity that flows from accepting in

"obedience of faith" God's gracious renewal of relationship. (Romans 3).

Conclusion: Paul's theological enterprise in Romans has its origins in his mature consideration of the twin problems of the inclusion of the Gentiles and the (apparent) self-exclusion of Israel from the promises of salvation. The distinctive theological vision of the letter emerged from his consideration of this problem within the light of his rich appreciation of the righteousness of God stemming from the Old Testament and apocalyptic tradition. In wrestling with the problem of God's seeming infidelity to Israel and his startling fidelity to the Gentiles, Paul elaborates a view of humanity stunted and ruinous, on the one hand, and humanity, renewed and pointed towards life, on the other. He sees these contrary effects as coming about entirely in terms of the essential relationship with God. He tells in Adam the story of human falling from relationship with God. He tells in Christ the story of human response to God's gracious offer of relationship. The gospel tells both stories as intertwined and lays the challenge: "You have been part of the Adam story; your human history is marked by its consequences. Do you wish to let the Christ story and its (more powerful) consequences be the final story told in your life and in your world?"

Romans is, then, a statement about God and a statement about humanity. It proclaims the paradox that the more human beings give glory to God, the more that glory redounds upon them to the enhancement of their own humanity. In this sense the *soli Deo gloria* becomes the *gloria Dei vivens homo* of Irenaeus. The focus and center of all is Christ, who embodies in his obedience both God's faithful and gracious offer of relationship and the archetypal human response.

The Gospel and Justice

In Romans we find comparatively little application of the gospel to concrete situations of human life. The exhortatory part of the letter, save for the controversial section on the state, remains on a fairly general level and is preoccupied for the most part with relationships within the Christian community. It is also true and to some extent notorious that in his more practical letters (e.g., 1 Corinthians) Paul makes no attempt to question or challenge social structures seemingly at odds with the view of human dignity emanating from his formulation of the gospel. In this connection, as we have already noted, the social status of women and the institution of slavery come immediately to mind. Paul's "social conservatism" in such respects doubtless stemmed from the keen eschatological sense that the "the outward frame of this world" was "passing away" (1 Cor 7:31). There was little point in the minuscule Christian community attempting to overthrow the established structures of a passing world. In this sense it is true that Paul hardly extended the social implications of the gospel beyond relationships between Christians themselves.

This does not mean, however, that Paul's gospel lacks relevance to the entire social question. On the contrary, the fact that he presents God's saving activity in Christ within the framework of the exercise of his righteousness means that the gospel is drawn out of the heart of God's total and faithful responsibility for creation. Paul's vision of Christ as the embodiment of God's saving fidelity to the world and his vision also that "in Christ" believers "become" the righteousness of God (2 Cor 5:21) means that to hear the gospel is to allow oneself to be built into that same total responsibility for the world.

God's whole exercise of righteousness in Christ is, as we have seen, directed to bringing human beings to the fullness of humanity and dignity that stems from being created in the image and likeness of God. This goal is achieved by the establishment of right relationships: firstly, the appropriate relationship between human beings and the Creator; secondly, the relationship of mutual acceptance between human groups that flows from this and is symbolized in Romans by the restored relationship between Israel and the Gentile world, prefigured in the Christian community. If a just social order is founded upon perception of human dignity and upon the structuring of relationships in such a way as to respect and enhance that dignity, then social justice has a radical theological foundation in Paul's gospel in Romans.

Moreover, Paul's subtle analysis of what holds human beings captive, his sense of what makes for dehumanization and destructiveness in relation to the created world sheds a penetrating light upon social and economic structures. Along with this is his sense that good intentions and any amount of moral effort cannot of themselves address the radical problem of human selfishness effectively. Liberation for growth to humanity is for Paul always the fruit of the Spirit, flowing from renewed relationship with God. In this sense Romans challenges any attempt to build a new world apart from reference to the Creator and acceptance in faith of his gracious involvement. It insists that Christ, in his obedience of total responsibility to the human, as well as in his resurrection glory, remains the touchstone of true humanity, of what it means to live a truly creative human life.

We may well ask what bearing these demands for explicit acknowledgment of God's gracious work in Christ have in a world where Christians make up only a proportion of the total population and that largely confined by historical circumstance to certain peoples and places. These are questions which Paul himself did not ask. But we can extend the direction of his thought as it emerges from the heart of Romans. Paul's sharp perception of the universalism of God's promise and his grace — the "Gentile" thrust, so to speak — urges us today to find the "shape" of the God of Romans present in all the genuine religious aspirations of human beings and indeed in all human attempts to surrender to mystery in sincerity and trust.

What Romans challenges is not so much other religions. It challenges all structures militating against true humanity, whether they be religious or not. It challenges all attempts to construct a future which does not take account of human beings as flawed, but graced, as contingent but chosen, as mortal, but destined, as enveloped in a mystery transcending present sight and understanding. The ultimate message of Romans is that God is and that he is "for us." Belief in God rightly construed is not "alienating." On the contrary, it is that which brings human beings home to themselves and each other as truly human.

READING:

*J.C. Beker, *Paul the Apostle* (Philadelphia: Fortress, 1980: London: SCM) 318-27.

N.A. Dahl, "The Doctrine of Justification: Its Social and Functional Implications," in *Studies in Paul* (Minneapolis: Augsburg, 1977) 95-120.

*J.R. Donahue, "Biblical Perspectives on Justice," in (J.C. Haughey, ed.) *The Faith that does Justice* (New York: Paulist, 1977) 68-112, esp. 88-103.

D. Dorr, *Option for the Poor: A Hundred Years of Vatican Social Teaching* (Dublin: Gill and Macmillan, 1983).

SUBJECT INDEX

228